# THE ART LIFE OF WILLIAM RIMMER

*Library of American Art*

# THE ART LIFE OF
# WILLIAM RIMMER

*Sculptor, Painter, and Physician*

By Truman H. Bartlett

New Preface by Leonard Baskin

*Kennedy Graphics, Inc. • Da Capo Press*
*New York • 1970*

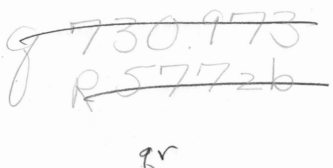
This edition of *The Art Life of William Rimmer* is an unabridged and corrected republication of the first edition published in Boston and New York in 1890. The publishers are grateful to the Museum of Fine Arts, Boston, and to the Fogg Art Museum, Harvard University, for providing new photographs for a number of illustrations.

Library of Congress Catalog Card Number 68-27718
SBN 306-71166-4

Published by Da Capo Press
A Division of Plenum Publishing Corporation
227 West 17th Street, New York, N.Y. 10011

# THE ART LIFE OF WILLIAM RIMMER

1.  ALEXANDER HAMILTON

# WILLIAM RIMMER: A NOTE

William Rimmer stands after Rush and Ward as the great American sculptor of the nine-teenth century, with the possible exception of Eakins, with whom he shared the calumny of the philistines and the obloquy of the academy. Given the man, his character and his train-ing, the corpus of his work is, to say it most mildly, miraculous. Rimmer infused his modelled figures with an astonishing power of forms. These forms are generated from within the sculp-ture and are vibrantly alive with the tension of force; a puissance bent to the meaning of the work. His great bronze *Dying Centaur* is massive and strong in the disposition of its forms, in the urgency of its thrust, the timelessness of its intention. Here is dying a gallant beast, a blessed Houyhnhnm. The work is free of flippant irrelevances, is not decorative, and it hearkens to an antique mold. Remarkable, for Rimmer was a naif, but transfixed with an archetypal sense of the monumental and grand in sculpture. He was the first American sculp-tor to carve stone directly. It was the fashion of fashionable and other sculptors to model a work in clay or wax and to present a plaster cast thereof to the professional stonecutter (in the nineteenth century usually at Carrara), who would pantographically carve the dead sim-ulacrum in marble. All of Rodin's marbles were thus achieved, which is why *eighty* ex-amples of the *Kiss* exist, all lifeless. When a sculptor carves, he is ever mindful of the usages of stone. His hand working the refractory material forges forms that are inimically marmo-real. It is of interest to note that not until the *twenties* of this century did sculptors begin to carve stones with their hands. The forsaken machines are employed now by academic sculp-tors for large projects.

Rimmer's statue of *Hamilton* stands on Commonwealth Avenue, at the approach to the Boston Public Garden. He probably had assistance in carving the work. The *Hamilton* has a contained silhouette, betraying its stoniness. The great domed head surmounts the stately figure, around which a robe improbably wraps. Every sculptor understands the incredible difficulty of dealing plastically with costume: buttons, shirtfronts, waistcoats, shoes, and buckles are disastrous. It can, with the greatest difficulty, be managed on an intimate scale

2.   ALEXANDER HAMILTON

3.   ALEXANDER HAMILTON

(Degas used an actual tutu), but monumentally it is an insoluble problem: ergo, togas, cloaks, capes, and wraps of all sorts are introduced to mask the sartorial trivia. Rimmer's wrap is somewhat too heavy, but the loss to felicity is small in light of the majesty and sense of immutability the sculpture gives, a requisite for all lasting monumental sculpture. Whenever I see the *Hamilton* I am continually impressed by the pervading and persuasive *presence* of the work. The great head of *St. Stephen* carved by Rimmer in granite compels our notice by the fierce turn of the head, the deep upturned eyes, the carapace-like skull; all bespeak the indomitable character of the stoned saint. Is Rimmer's *Stephen* the first granite carving in America? I rather think so.

As I remember them, Rimmer's paintings are far less realized as works of art, although his painting *Pursuit* is wondrous. It belongs in that company of paintings which seize upon a psychological state, terror or anxiety, the effects of nightmare, and graphically illumine that state. Fuseli's *Nightmare* is such a picture. Rimmer's *Pursuit* exists in hallucinatory space and time, the pursuit is endless and simultaneous, and in viewing it, we are warped into the dream's foreboding sphere.

Rimmer and Eakins, presumably unknown to one another, were near berserk in the love of anatomy. Both suffered the canting caterwauling of hysterical school boards. But anatomy is a private passion. In the cellar of the Pennsylvania Academy of Fine Arts stands a barrel filled with anatomical molds, painted to simulate muscle and tissue, while nearby is a stained plaster cast of a flayed cat and two great bronzes of the articulated corpse of a Philadelphia longshoreman — all prepared by Eakins. What secret anatomical excess remains hid in Rimmer's forgotten cabinet, one cannot say, but we do have, to study and to ponder, his wonderful *Art Anatomy*. It is extraordinary that Rimmer could so force his brain and hand to consummately master and masterfully render the entire mystery of subcutaneous anatomy. One could trace many a source for the drawings, and see observed in Rimmer's anatomy notions from Theophrastus, Camper, and Lavater. The *Art Anatomy* is so well known and currently available in dead offset, that it would be useless for me to bespeak its qualities. It is a great artistic document of nineteenth-century·American art.

Rimmer's life and work come to compelling life in Bartlett's book. The republication of Bartlett will spur the installation of Rimmer to fame and understanding. For an artist so denied, so objured, whose repute and esteem were driven to dust, to emerge from the submerged mass of irrelevance is heartening testimony that truth prismed by style contains its ultimate triumph and that ephemeral celebrations void of truth sink out of sight, with a moan.

*Little Deer Isle, Maine*                                                                          Leonard Baskin
*8 July 1968*

Rimmer at the Age of Fifty

# THE ART LIFE OF

# WILLIAM RIMMER

## Sculptor, Painter, and Physician

BY

TRUMAN H. BARTLETT

SCULPTOR

BOSTON AND NEW YORK

HOUGHTON, MIFFLIN AND COMPANY

The Riverside Press, Cambridge

1890

"*But genius itself, whose likeness is terrible and unlovely at first sight to the run of men, filling them with affright and scandal — with wonder and the repellent sense, that a new and strange thing is brought into the world.*"

SWINBURNE.

"*Truth is always in the extremes, — keep them.*"

WILLIAM BLAKE.

"*Man is a skeleton of which the muscles are the ornament.*"

RUDE.

# INTRODUCTION.

D R. WILLIAM RIMMER, the subject of the following sketch, was well known in art circles in Boston for the eighteen years preceding his death in 1879, as a remarkable lecturer upon art anatomy, a skilful delineator of its forms, as the sculptor of several statues and busts, and as a man who had painted much without establishing a reputation as a painter. For four years, included in this period, he was also known in New York as the director of the School of Design for Women at the Cooper Institute.

Of his origin nothing whatever was learned, either by his friends or the public; and outside of his family-circle little was known of his life or his struggles, even by his immediate friends.

His plaster statue of THE FALLING GLADIATOR, when in 1861 it was first shown at his house in East Milton, and soon after in Boston, was pronounced a remarkable work, and its author a modern Michael Angelo. But neither this work, nor the ST. STEPHEN, which was produced a year earlier, gained at that time the place in public esteem which they merited; and, after a temporary success, both sank into undeserved obscurity.

In May, 1880, an exhibition of Dr. Rimmer's works, consisting of sculptures, paintings, and drawings, was opened at the Boston Art Museum. Many even among his pupils were astonished at the variety and imaginative character of this collection. Such fertility, such rare and profound intuitive knowledge, so great comprehension of composition, had never before been seen in the works of an American artist. Death awakens and increases human interest for the moment at least, and compels an explanation of the existence of beings who have in their lives baffled human curiosity. Over the works shown after Dr. Rimmer's death were uttered question and comment the most varied and conflicting, and the most widely differing theories and estimates were spoken.

To answer in some degree these questions, to give some account of the artist and his work, is the aim of this sketch. It is only after much hesitation that his family consented to the publication of any facts concerning his origin or his life. They not only preferred to cherish apart their remembrance and their sorrow, but they desired to respect his habit of reticence, and his often-expressed wish that after death his history might remain shrouded in the obscurity which enveloped it in life.

Upon the consideration, however, that in a certain sense her husband belonged to the world, and that artists especially had a right to know something of his art-life, Mrs. Rimmer consented to give such information as she thought proper toward the accomplishment of the purpose of this book. She allowed also the free use of the drawings in her possession, from which the illustrations are taken.

To Mrs. Rimmer, for her kindness in permitting the use of the material, and to her daughter Miss Caroline H. Rimmer, for her cheerful labor in assisting in its preparation, my grateful acknowledgments are presented.

A circular requesting any available information was sent to all the pupils, friends, or acquaintances of Dr. Rimmer's whose names could be ascertained; and, in reply to about five hundred circulars, one hundred and fifty answers were received, relating facts in his history as far back as 1824. It is significant that several persons prominently connected with art, in the principal localities where Dr. Rimmer worked and lectured, wrote that they did not know him. The majority of the replies came from the doctor's pupils, and were interesting, not only as assisting in the accomplishment of my purpose, but as records of impressions, susceptibilities, perceptions, and memories of persons brought under the influence of a powerful art nature. A man's work is himself: on whatever he touches, whether stone, color, pencil, or human hearts, everywhere is left the record of his true being.

I was also able to find people who had been acquainted with William Rimmer in his boyhood, youth, manhood, and later life; and to gain very full information of at least the outward aspect of his career.

Every one will appreciate the difficulties of attempting to give a full account of any phase of the life of a person so lately deceased. Many facts of interest and importance, proper to be stated in another generation, cannot now be appropriately recorded.

To those who have so kindly and laboriously assisted me with valuable material, and have expressed such appreciative interest in this undertaking, I give my sincere thanks.

# CONTENTS.

# LIST OF ILLUSTRATIONS

# THE ART LIFE OF WILLIAM RIMMER.

## CHAPTER I.

### THOMAS RIMMER. — EARLY LIFE OF WILLIAM.

#### 1816-1833.

CRISPIN chronicler relates, that, "some time in the year 1824, there appeared in the quiet and rural shoemaking town of Hopkinton, Mass., an unusually good workman, who was able to take the leather in the rough, and make a very nice sewed boot, doing all the work himself, and excelling in all parts of his trade. He did not remain in town more than three months; and one day, after finishing a pair of boots, he said, 'It is time for me to go West,' and off he went."

A fellow-workman adds, "That English shoemaker could do every thing. He was a travelling wonder for those staid times. He made his own tools, fenced, boxed, and played different musical instruments. He knew more than his employers; and I always thought he must have a strange history, and that he had been used to something better than shoemaking. He was a restless mortal, and it did not take him long to make the circuit of all the workshops in the vicinity of Boston. He was known as the 'tramping jour.'"

This was Thomas Rimmer, father of Dr. William Rimmer, the subject of this sketch.

Thomas Rimmer belonged to a branch of one of the royal families of France. Born during the revolution of 1789, he was reared from his infancy in the utmost seclusion in England, in the home of an English family. Until he became a youth, he supposed himself a member of the family in which he lived, although he enjoyed luxuries, received instruction in accomplishments, and was treated with distinctions, which the other children of the family did not share. A love for military life developed itself in him at an early age, and at length became his dominant thought. When he was informed of his distinguished origin, the position which he was destined to occupy, and the princely inheritance which should eventually become his, he gave full rein to his military ardor, and centred all his ambition upon the life of a soldier. Opposed in his wishes by those having him in charge, he ran away, and joined the English army. He aspired to win a name, and to deserve a place among the chivalrous spirits with whom he expected to associate in an early future.

Distinction, with royal favor, was almost within his possession, when political and family complications suddenly arose; and the young soldier found his inheritance wrongfully taken from him, and soon discovered, too, that neither his birthright nor name would avail him any thing in the scale of justice.

Proud, hot-blooded, and sensitive, he threw up his commission, leaving the army and the country in rage and despair, and sailed for Nova Scotia, where he landed in 1818. Determined to be forever done with the old life, he abandoned even his name, concealing his identity under the assumed title " Thomas Rimmer," and selecting the trade of a shoemaker as being the means of earning a livelihood which would be likely to bring him least in contact with his fellow-men.

Soon after his arrival, he sent for his wife, Mrs. Mary Rimmer, an Irish lady, and for his only child, William, born at Liverpool, Eng., Feb. 20, 1816.

To hide himself from mankind had been the fixed determination of Thomas Rimmer when he left the Old World for the New; and in this resolve he never wavered, seeking all his enjoyment in the exercise of his varied accomplishments and in the pleasures of his hearthstone. The memory of the thwarted hopes of his happy boyhood, and of the injustice which had blighted his life, became ever more acute and bitter as years went on; and the feelings which they engendered were shared by William as soon as the boy became old enough to understand them. A distrust of men, a keen realization of human injustice, and the consciousness of the ever-pursuing shadow of an untoward fate, were the earliest impressions of Dr. Rimmer's childhood,—impressions which later experiences only strengthened. The cruel uncertainties of an ambitious life are hard enough for

5. DESPAIR

4. THOMAS RIMMER

the bravest and strongest to bear under the most favorable of earthly conditions; but what a spirit of steel does he not need, who, born with the love of life for life's sake, and full of high hopes, finds the splendid future, which had seemed actually within his grasp, suddenly wrested from him by strong-handed injustice! All that the father had suffered had a scarcely less direct effect upon the son than its actual experience would have had; and, while still a boy in years, William was in feeling a wronged and saddened man.

An artistic tendency showed itself in the child William before he was out of pinafores; his first expression of this being to cut up an entire chintz bedquilt into butterflies, without telling any one of his performance. His parents were rather pleased, than otherwise, with this unusual transformation of utility into a representation of the sacred but short-lived insect, and encouraged the boy's creative fancies. The first snow which fell after the making of the chintz butterflies was shaped by the youthful artist into mimic soldiers; shoemaker's wax his small fingers drew and twisted into dragons and other frightful beasts; while it only needed the aid of a penknife to transform bits of chalk into equally strange and fanciful forms.

In 1826, when William was ten years of age, the Rimmer family came to Boston, and lived for a few years in a little unnamed street still existing, and leading off Federal Street, opposite what is now Wales's Wharf. On the wharf was a granite-yard and a storehouse for gypsum; and one who was playmate of William at this time, and comrade for many years after, relates that his friend used to cut from the gypsum and alabaster figures as large as himself.

Leaving the vicinity of Wales's Wharf, the Rimmers moved to C Street, South Boston, — a locality as retired as any in the city. The father was known among his neighbors as a strange man, with varied and wonderful powers, a quick temper, and a strong fist, who kept himself aloof, and had evidently seen better days. The family, indeed, were scarcely less isolated from men than had they lived in a Western wilderness. There were, by this time, seven children, — six boys and one girl; and it was the father's purpose himself to instruct them in whatever of knowledge or accomplishment he possessed. He was a man of many parts; by nature of fine feeling and generous temper, and having a wonderful facility for accomplishing whatever he chose to undertake. He drew and painted skilfully, and was familiar with art and with scientific and literary topics. His children all showed more or less talent for art, — a fact from which he derived much gratification; and he did all in his power to foster and develop their powers.

As soon as the boys were old enough, they assisted their father at his trade ; and although shoemaking was not productive of a luxurious or certain income, yet by hard and steady work the Rimmers were not only able to obtain a living, but to save something wherewith to purchase books, colors, and other necessities of art and educational progress. The boys studied as they worked at the bench ; and the rare half-holidays were devoted to drawing, painting, or to long tramps into the woods to gather flowers and to study plants ; botany and ornithology being included in their list of studies. How incongruous was the position of Thomas Rimmer is strikingly illustrated by the education he gave to his boys, as well as by the fact that he experimented in the raising of silkworms, in electricity and metallurgy. He also made musical instruments, and each child had a flute adapted to his special voice.

In their sunny days the Rimmers danced and sung, fenced and fished, painted and drew, and made their humble life joyous. They gave concerts by themselves, the children being arranged in order, according to their age and height, the tallest in the rear, while the father conducted with the dignity and severity of an exacting leader.

The shoemaker's house on C Street was a domestic academy of the fine arts ; its professor a nobleman, and its pupils his own flesh and blood. Often the nights were spent in labor, that the entire day might be given to outdoor study or recreation. The evenings, when not given to music, were enlivened with declamation, or to some exercise for mutual improvement. History was read ; the stories of great battles recited and illustrated with ready fancy and skilful pencils. With such a training, it is not strange that biblical and historical scenes were the common subjects for illustration and symbolic representation with Dr. Rimmer throughout his whole life. All the joy of William's boyhood was centred in his home ; and in manhood and age it was still in the domestic circle that he found his supreme happiness.

But there came dark days also. The responsibilities of a large family, the constantly increasing sting of old memories, re-awakened by the sight of the youth of his boys, began to tell upon Thomas Rimmer. Some of the boys, and especially William, were giving striking indications of at least unusual talent ; and the impossibility of fostering these natural gifts still more imbittered the father. Days of desperation became often days of dissipation ; and to the children there came scenes and shadows which were never effaced. Thomas Rimmer had, when excited, a terrible temper. One who knew him at that time relates the following incident : —

"Rimmer was," he says, "for those days — or, indeed, for these — a strange man.

7. MIDNIGHT RIDE

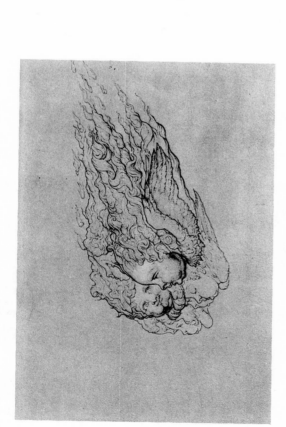

6. SHOOTING STARS

9. FALLING FIGURES

8. LANDSCAPE

He used to go off by himself on the shore, and sit for hours looking out to sea. He kept by himself, for the most part; but there were times when he made things pretty hot! He owned a fine flute, which on one occasion he loaned to a neighbor, who refused to return it. The owner swore that if it were not returned there would be trouble; and there was trouble, for he had a terrible temper, and would have fought all South Boston in defence of what he regarded as his rights. He went into the house of the man who had the flute, and was obliged to whip him and all his friends before he could regain his property. It was a terrible row."

The seclusion in which the family lived did not wholly prevent young Rimmer from forming youthful friendships, and he seems to have impressed all of his boyish acquaintances as a person of unusual and singular character. One of them says, " He became celebrated as the boy who made India-rubber horses. He cut them with his knife from the soles of discarded overshoes, the legs being always well attached; and half the boys in the neighborhood were continually ransacking the streets of Boston for old rubbers for Bill Rimmer to make into horses. He was at the head, too, of a boat-club. The boys built their own boats; Rimmer making the designs, and assigning to each his part of the labor, and always showing a wonderful knowledge of what each boy could do. He seemed able to do any thing, and always led. There was no end to his activity, and he worked night and day."

His home-life had a strong and lasting influence upon the genius of William. From their historical and legendary talks resulted that admiration and fondness for warriors and mighty men which awakened his sensibilities into so powerful action in his boyhood, and which he never lost. The loneliness and isolation of their home undoubtedly had much to do with the remoteness from actual life which is so powerfully marked in his art development. Distance was ever to him an enchantment; characters of undisturbed dignity in history, for instance, appearing to him as veritable gods. The idea of struggle against a stern fate, so common in his drawings, is the inevitable outcome of that conflict with untoward circumstances which he knew so young; the foregoing of comfort to gain some coveted indulgence in the products of rare minds. Varied and pathetic pictures were those which made up the boy's youth, contrasting sharply with the elegant, luxurious boyhood of his father.

As has been before observed, William became the sympathetic inheritor of his father's early history, and, at the age of fourteen, to a large extent the responsible member and reliable support of the family. When other boys were rejoicing in the joys of careless, happy youth, William Rimmer was carrying on his boyish shoulders the grave responsibilities of a man.

To earn more than was possible by mere manual labor, and to follow the occupation which was most congenial to his taste, he started out at the age of fifteen as a painter of portraits, signs, or other pictures, and as a draughtsman. By the aid of some influential friend whose notice had been attracted by his unusual talents, he secured a place in a studio on Boylston Street; but this arrangement was of no great duration. For portraits he received from five to twenty dollars each. No trace of any of the work done at this time can be found, with the single exception of a little sitting figure carved in gypsum, when he was fifteen. It was studied from life, and represents his father's physical and mental characteristics. It is DESPAIR. Of all the works left by Dr. Rimmer, this is one of the most interesting and significant, possibly the most so. The vivid comprehension of his father's mental condition; the idea, mutually considered and adopted, of expressing it in sculpture; the compact and forcible conception of the idea; and the vital temperament of a sculptor which it exhibits in its execution, — make it not only the first and only piece of real primitive sculpture executed in America, but give to it so extraordinary an individuality, that the credulity is even taxed to believe the facts of its production. It is hardly necessary to add that no other sculptor on this continent has shown so much of the sculptor's temperament as is indicated in this figure. It shows the frankest loyalty to the model, a wonderful concentration in the composition of the figure, and a natural genius for expression. The two latter qualities characterize all of Dr. Rimmer's work. As he grew older, nature, as felt in this figure, became subordinate to the imagination, to knowledge, to construction. Whether this was due to the dominating power of his imagination, and an indifference to the employment of living models, or in some degree to the difficulty of obtaining models at all satisfactory, it is not easy to determine. It is true, however, that when he was before the public as a sculptor, from 1861 to 1879, the facilities for obtaining models were much better, and he employed them but little, and then only for references.

Of the many other statuettes which the young artist cut in gypsum, nothing is remembered but the subjects. They, for the most part, symbolized the facts or sentiments of his own or his father's life, either by the conquered or conquering ideal figure of a warrior. Some of these were exhibited as late as 1838 in Colton's art-store on Tremont Street, and were " well received," as the doctor said many years afterward; though whether this favorable reception was limited to compliments, or extended to purchase, he did not state.

It is significant, too, that of all the figures cut by young Rimmer, before and after the execution of DESPAIR, this alone should have been preserved, remaining a lonely, mocking reminder to its author that he also must ever gather himself up in lonely anguish, vainly hoping for any consummation of his hopes in this world.

## CHAPTER II.

### YOUTHFUL STRUGGLES.

#### 1830–1840.

THE young artist's first experiment in supporting himself and aiding his father by the practice of art not proving sufficiently remunerative, he tried a variety of occupations in the hope of obtaining a livelihood. Between the ages of fifteen and twenty-one, we find him type-setting, soap-making, working in India-rubber, painting signs, and employed in a lithographic establishment.

A brother artist, who was one of his youthful comrades, writes as follows of Rimmer's connection with the art of lithography: "I became acquainted with Dr. Rimmer when I was connected with Moore's lithographic establishment. He came there as a student in the art, and remained about a year, doing the drudgery of the establishment. We were in the same room. He always took part in the discussions on art matters which were constantly going on among the students; and, while many of his notions were crude, his perceptions and aspirations were far above those of the others. I had a high estimate of his mental abilities, and felt, that, if he could have a chance, he would develop into an artist far above the ordinary.

"When and where he became possessed of the grand and elevated ideas of art he afterward developed, I can hardly imagine, though I believe the germs were in his nature from the first. Up to this time, at least, I am not aware that he had received any instruction in art unless at home. He had a certain knowledge of anatomy; and, when criticised because he drew certain muscles in a manner different from that practised in the establishment, he would say, 'I know my way is right, for I saw it in such an Anatomy.' We thought his drawings exaggerated,

8

but he always defended them. Looking back to that time, I can see that he was already formulating his ideas for practical work. He had painted heads and ornaments, and I remember distinctly a head that he dashed off in a splendid manner. Its tone was low, and its treatment harmonious.

"I recall two of his lithographic designs. One represented a scene upon a snowy mountain-side, where the body of a frozen shepherd was defended from an eagle by his faithful dog. The other was the title-page of a piece of music entitled 'The Fireman's Call.' In this he depicted a fireman rushing from a burning building, bearing in his arms a woman and her child; and the design had much of the *verve* and dash which characterized his later work."

At the end of the year work failed in the lithographic house, and young Rimmer formed a partnership with Elbridge Harris to paint signs and decorative work. Their advertising card was an immense picture of CROMWELL AT THE BATTLE OF MARSTON MOOR, which they displayed upon the front of their shop on Washington Street, nearly opposite the Old South, This partnership did not endure long, perhaps the most important thing about it being the sensation which was caused by the sign. Staid Boston had never seen any thing of the kind used for such a purpose. The picture was painted in the brightest colors, with great masses of yellow and red; and it is remembered that Rimmer's associates thought the work had, to quote their expression, "lots of good stuff in it."

The artist's next move was to take a studio on School Street, where he painted a number of pictures on religious subjects for the Endicott-street Catholic Church, and for other chapels in the vicinity of Boston. The Catholic priests were thus the first, and for a long time the most important, patrons of the young painter.

Rimmer at this time was a wiry, athletic young man, with thin muscular development, and rather proud of his strength. His physical bravery was beyond limit, although his companions thought him deficient in both moral courage and in perseverance. He wore commonly tight-fitting black trousers, a bottle-green coat with brass buttons, fastened so high at the throat as to leave nothing of shirt-front or vest visible. His conversational voice was on a low key, rich, deep, and harmonious; and he sang a magnificent bass. During working-hours any room where he was employed was always ringing with snatches of song, usually bits from oratorios, or other choice works.

Of Rimmer's voice all his friends speak with the utmost admiration. He sang in the Methodist church on Church Street; was a member of the Boston Musical Institute, and of a singing-society which met in Mozart Hall.   He also belonged to a serenading club that at one time sang on the Common nightly until the police, for some unknown reason, interfered.   His great diffidence, however, prevented his making his musical talents of much practical use.   Some of his friends, convinced that such a bass voice was worth a fortune, encouraged him to sing at the theatre; and, after much solicitation he consented to appear.   The evening came, and so did the hour: but Rimmer could not be found; his courage was not equal to the ordeal.

His varied life had by this time greatly enlarged his circle of acquaintances; and, although all were prevented by his persistent reserve from any thing like familiar intimacy, he yet had many associates of his own age.   He joined Fire-Engine Company No. 12, the City Guards, and the musical organizations already mentioned.

In connection with his membership with the first of these, the following incident is told by one of his associates: " A crowd of us once went to a large fire in Cambridge, Bill Rimmer and his brother Tom being of the number.   We were assisting in tearing down a burning wooden building when one side suddenly fell, and a man was caught between the timbers.   It was an awful sight.   Rimmer thought it was his brother Tom, and rushed into the flames to save him.   We all tried to help, but it was of no use.   We could not lift the burning side of a building, and we were forced to rush back to save our own lives.   Rimmer remained, and would have been burned, had not Tom appeared at that moment safe and sound.   The incident created much talk about town, although the public generally did not know who risked his life to save another.   Not long after, Rimmer and I were standing on the street together, when a man whom I knew slightly came along, and recounted the story as if he were the hero.   During the recital Rimmer said not a word; but after the man moved away he exclaimed, with much force, ' What a liar!' "

He was very fond of the society of ladies, and very likely utilized his connection with the serenading club as a means of advancing in their good graces, — a proceeding much more in keeping with the spirit of that time than of the present.   For we are writing of the days when " Old Reed" the constable, with his heavy cane and red neck-handkerchief, was the terror of evil-doers throughout the town; when Wilson the town-crier, with his big bell and " Child lost!" startled mothers with fears for the safety of their own broods; when " big Dick," the negro pugilist, was the model about whom centred the admiration and ambition of all the schoolboys; when the regular Saturday-night fire-alarm started out with singular promptness, and exactly one hundred men on the rope, with songs, noise of horns, yells, and clamor enough to raise the

10. THE HUNTER'S DOG

11. EMPEROR, WARRIOR AND POET

12. SOOTHSAYER

dead; when the fights between North and South Enders were frequent and furious, and the fun of election and training days on the Common was the delight of all the riotous youngsters in the town. From all this life Rimmer undoubtedly gained more than most of his companions: but art had no proper place or recognition; and it was in the face of innumerable obstacles, not the least of which was the general public indifference, that the young artist made his way.

About his family Rimmer never talked with his friends, and his reticence and strange nature threw about him an air of mystery which his associates felt strongly. He had small power of adapting himself to people, while his fickleness and arrogance made him most unpopular. His superior mind and accomplishments saved him many friends, who but for these would have shunned him. He was uncompromising and defiant, and tried their patience almost beyond endurance, injuring himself recklessly, and seeming incapable of what is familiarly known as "wire-pulling."

An old acquaintance tells of an important art enterprise in which he was a partner with young Rimmer, and which belongs properly to this part of our story.

"I think it was in 1838 or '39," he says, "that I was passing with Rimmer along Tremont Row, where a picture called *Cain and Abel* was on exhibition. It attracted much attention, and was bringing in considerable money to those exhibiting it. Rimmer said to me, 'If I had a chance, I could paint a picture as good as that one.' I asked him why he did not do it, and make some money; for at that time he was out of both funds and employment. 'I can't raise the money for the necessary expenses of such an undertaking,' he replied. I told him I would furnish the means of carrying out the scheme, if he would undertake the work, with the understanding that we were to share alike in the profits. He accepted the offer. A large room in the Thorndyke Building on Tremont Row was hired, the necessary material procured, and he set to work. The canvas must have been eight feet square. Rimmer worked like a tiger. It was a pleasure to see him. He called his picture AFTER THE DEATH OF ABEL; and it represented Adam and Eve mourning over the dead body of their son. He was very particular about the figure of Eve, and we had no end of trouble in finding the right model. I remember going in one morning, and finding eight nude female models standing in a row. I was never more surprised in my life, and the women appeared surprised also. Rimmer at length selected one or two, and dismissed the others.

"I watched the progress of the work, and paid the bills, Rimmer's personal expenses included. No one could have worked harder than he did for six or eight weeks. He purposed at first painting Eve perfectly nude but feared that this would offend public prejudice, and therefore gave her certain draperies which one of his friends said looked like a door-mat. 'It ought to,' Rimmer responded: 'it was painted from one.'

"The picture was at length completed, and placed upon exhibition in the room where it was painted, an entrance fee of twenty-five cents being charged to visitors, of whom there were a good many. The color was not pleasing; and although it had many merits, perhaps more than were recognized, it was not a success so far as money was concerned. Rimmer lost his time, and I was out sixty dollars. The disappointment was a severe one to Rimmer, and he felt it deeply. I was very sorry for him; for I thought him a man of unusual ability, who ought to have a chance to work out what was in him. I afterward sold the picture to the Lowell Museum, and it was burned with that institution. My loss troubled him, although he was in no way to blame. From the time this transaction ended, I did not speak with him for nearly thirty years. Occasionally I saw him on the street, sometimes approaching, but he was sure to cross to the other side before we could meet. Knowing his nature, I understood what all this meant. He did not wish to speak to me. His likes and dislikes were very strong; and he would cut an old friend or acquaintance dead, for reasons or without, if he happened to fancy. Sometimes, in such a case, he would eventually come round all right, and be as friendly as ever. I paid no attention to his desire to avoid me, for I cared nothing about it; and it must have been twenty-odd years later that I read in the papers something about a Dr. Rimmer. From time to time there were notices of the same person in one public connection or another, until, some time in the seventies, I heard that he had a school in Bromfield Street. Passing this place one day, I thought I would go up and see if it were the Bill Rimmer of the old times. I hoped it might be, and that he had become prosperous and famous. I mounted the stairs, found the door, and knocked. A voice, which I recognized at once, called out, 'Come in!' I opened the door, walked in, and saw Rimmer painting a large landscape with figures. 'Bill,' I said before he could turn, 'your color hasn't improved much in thirty years.' He wheeled about with a look, which, had it been translated into action, would have pitched me down stairs; but, recognizing my face, he grasped my hand, expressed his pleasure at seeing me, made me sit down, and we soon were talking over the old days in a most delightful manner. He seemed to enjoy it as much as I: the 'Abel' picture was painted over again, and for two hours the past thirty-five years appeared as yesterday.

"Rimmer could not have been more than twenty when he painted AFTER THE DEATH OF ABEL. He worked with great rapidity, whipping a picture into shape in an astonishingly short time. Battle scenes he drew with wonderful facility. His figures were always antique, and he had no wish to be influenced by any thing about him. I never saw any one who worked so hard. He actually worked and wept."

# CHAPTER III.

### BROCKTON. — RANDOLPH. — SOUTH BOSTON AND BOSTON.

### 1840-1845.

THE ten years of Rimmer's life between 1830 and 1840 embraced his first acquaintance with the world, his first public efforts in art, and his first experience, in many ways, to assist his father and push his own fortunes. His art efforts were not successful as compared with those of the popular artists of that day. What merits his paintings possessed, it is impossible to determine; for I have been unable to find a single specimen belonging to this period. There is no record of his having employed any of the methods common to enterprising young artists. He made neither busts nor portraits of the principal public men, nor is it known that he was acquainted with any of them. If his pictures were like those afterward painted in Brockton and Randolph, it is not surprising that they did not win recognition for the young painter; since the merits of these were not of a kind likely to please the public then, as, indeed, they would hardly do now. Evidently the artist recommended himself to public consideration neither by himself nor by his work. He must seek some other means of subsistence, and some other outlet to his talents.

If his other gypsum statuettes were as good as the one already described, or better, — for it is reasonable to suppose that he made some progress, — it would appear strange that they did not win for the sculptor some momentary, if not permanent, encouragement. Young men who were showing the slightest capability for art, in different parts of the country, were receiving generous encouragement. Powers, in Cincinnati, after making busts by the dozen, was wafted to Italy in 1837 by the good wishes of almost a national interest in art; Clark Mills was in the South, receiving orders for more work than he could execute; Crawford, Brown,

14

Page, Huntington, and others were finding the road to fortune by the aid of enthusiastic and powerful friends and a voyage to Italy; and Horatio Greenough was already in that favored land.

Of the condition of things in Boston, an old artist writes: " Allston was living in Cambridge in a very retired way, but accessible and kindly in his reception of young artists seeking information; although most of the young men were reluctant about troubling him, because he seemed so far away and above them. He stood alone, — a genius apart. I saw him at various times in picture exhibitions, and listened to his delightful words. The famous exhibition of all his accessible works, in 1837 or 1838, gave me more pleasure than almost any other I have seen by more renowned men. Chester Harding was painting in Boston, and was the portrait-painter *par excellence* of that time. I remember that H. K. Brown came to Boston, and modelled a few busts, and seemed to infuse a new life into the dull art-circles by his enthusiasm; but he soon left. Albert Hoyt was just beginning to be known by some carefully drawn and truthful portraits. William Page also came to Boston at this period, and remained for a time, making quite a sensation with one or two pictures. One was the 'Holy Family,' now in the Museum of Fine Arts, I think. He also showed a number of heads, among them the John Quincy Adams portrait, now so well known. Alvin Fisher was a successful local artist, who painted pleasing pictures of all subjects, landscape, portrait, and animal; George L. Brown had already commenced his career; Thomas Doughty was also in Boston; S. L. Gerry, a decorative painter, was just beginning to paint landscapes; Ball Hughes had made his group of 'Uncle Toby and Widow Wadman;' Francis Alexander, Benjamin Champney, and, I think, Allan Gay, were also of Rimmer's time. Later on came R. M. Staigg, Joseph Ames, Thomas Ball, Pratt, Hollingsworth, and Carleton.

"There were no facilities for studying art in Boston, — neither school nor masters. All the knowledge that Rimmer or the rest of us acquired was from books, nature, Allston, and the Athenæum. The plaster casts were in the gallery of the latter. A few of us used to get together, and draw from reduced copies of the antique statues. I think Rimmer was not one of our number."

The last sentence of the above explains to a certain extent Rimmer's position in Boston, so far as the artists were concerned. It was his nature to keep aloof from any general intimacy with the members of his profession; and his acquaintance with them, during any period of his life, was limited. If there was any advantage to be derived from association with them, he voluntarily neglected to avail himself of it. A young man who thought as he did, and could do as he did in the figure of DESPAIR, would naturally find little interest in the efforts of the artists of his day. He went his own independent way among the artists and those who were patronizing art.

Throughout Dr. Rimmer's life the domestic dominated the art side of his nature. His home was his world. It is an old saying, that the art instinct neither submits to, nor permits, a rival. It was as true in his case as it had been in similar ones, and had much to do with the unevenness of his art career.

In 1840 William Rimmer married Miss Mary H. C. Peabody, a Quakeress, and soon after started on a tour of portrait-painting through the towns of Randolph, Norfolk County, and Brockton (then Bridgewater) in Plymouth County, Mass. From the above date to 1845, when he settled permanently in the first-named town as a shoemaker, he was working alternately in those places and in Boston. His success was, on the whole, pretty satisfactory; although at the time of his marriage he was seriously considering the plan of studying medicine as a more certain means of support. In Brockton he made the acquaintance of Dr. A. W. Kingman, whose hospitality he shared, and whose friendship he enjoyed as long as he lived. When at length he decided to become a physician, moreover, he found in Dr. Kingman's library the medical works that he wished to study, and in the doctor a good adviser and teacher.

Upon the people of Brockton, Rimmer made the same impression which followed him everywhere, — of being an original, self-centred, and erratic man, possessed both of great natural powers and large attainments. He was always a brilliant and tireless talker, advancing constantly the most startling and beautiful theories, and making astonishing statements, often with the most reckless disregard alike of the opinions and feelings of his hearers. Ordinary people were able neither to follow nor to understand him, and it naturally resulted that they were often half in doubt of his sanity. He seems to have enjoyed their bewilderment, and very likely sometimes amused himself by purposely increasing it. He differed radically from the prevalent religious belief in Brockton, and although speaking upon this subject with prudence, he still aroused much antagonism. He was perfectly aware that he was unpopular, and made little effort to soften dislikes or to conciliate. He either did not care for human affinities, or steeled himself to do without them. He was kind and affectionate with the children; giving them drawings and making pictures for them, for which they always remembered him.

He judged men with perfect accuracy. He would often take as a subject for illustration some person who attracted his attention, and make a drawing of him, going through an exacting analysis of his character and tendencies. Then he would select some leading trait of the man, and draw a figure dominated by that trait, and tell what such a being would be likely to think about. He incurred the especial dislike of a certain clergyman by subjecting his character to such a treatment; thereby increasing an existing dislike of which he was aware, but which he felt to be unjust.

While at Brockton he painted many portraits, among them those of Dr. Kingman's father, a gentleman seventy-five years of age, and a large picture of Dr. Kingman, grouped with his wife and four children. A gentleman relates that he was once in Dr. Rimmer's studio, when a lady called, and expressed her dissatisfaction of her portrait, which was standing unfinished upon the easel. Turning her back upon the artist, she began explaining her objections to the caller. While she was speaking, Rimmer drew with great rapidity over the face of the portrait a long train of monkeys in all sorts of extravagant positions. The lady's surprise and annoyance when, on turning again toward the picture, she saw her counterfeit presentment so ornamented, may be readily imagined; but the difficulty was finally arranged, and the work rendered satisfactory.

Painting solely as a means of livelihood, Rimmer would work for any price offered; declaring, in answer to the advice of a friend to do well whatever he·did at all, " I had as lief paint a picture for five as for fifty dollars, and shall give of my work just in proportion to the amount I receive." Working upon this principle, he not infrequently painted a portrait for five or ten dollars, and finished it up in a single half-day.

The only pictures by Dr. Rimmer, painted in Brockton, that I have succeeded in finding, are the Kingman portraits. The life-sized portrait, of head and shoulders, of Dr. Kingman's father, is now — forty years after its execution — very thin and dry as a painting, although the color is tender, and the head well constructed. The family picture not only lacks every merit desirable in a work of art, but it is as awkward in its arrangement as could well be imagined. It is surprising that it should not indicate, even in a slight degree, some of the powerful art qualities that the artist abundantly possessed  It is still more surprising that he should have permitted such a picture to exist anywhere, and especially in the home of one of his best friends, as a greeting to himself whenever he visited at Dr. Kingman's, — a pleasure which he enjoyed annually until a few years before his death.

Having decided to become a physician, Rimmer gave all the time not occupied in painting to the study of his chosen profession. Dr. Kingman heard him recite twice a week, giving him at all times every assistance that lay in his power. Rimmer had already much knowledge of some branches of the subject, especially of anatomy. The two men were fast friends, Dr. Kingman enjoying and appreciating the other's artistic nature and brilliant talk. "We could agree about nothing," Dr. Kingman says, "but we were happy in disagreeing. He impressed me more than any person I ever knew as an original mind. Our conversations concerned the powers of observation, perception, the internal recognition of things, rather than arguments about creeds and beliefs. I never knew any thing about his origin, but often thought it must be of some strange nature. He never mentioned the subject. He visited me several times a year, until a short time before his death, generally remaining over night; and we talked all the time we were together. On one of his visits he was full of spiritualism, and proposed to get a message from my father. Taking a pencil in his hand, he held it in the air for a moment, then it began to descend toward the table, and finally to write. This movement was repeated several times until quite a lot of senseless stuff was written. I said, 'Nonsense, Rimmer!' The expression hurt him, though he made no response.

"Human relationship outside of his family did not seem to affect him, or occupy his attention. Why he went to East Milton to practise, I cannot imagine; possibly because he wished to get a little experience before going into a larger field.

"He was an enchanting talker, and impressed me as one who — if he could have had good, fair opportunities in his youth — would have made a most remarkable man."

Some time between the years 1840 and 1845, and after he had begun his medical studies, Dr. Rimmer lived for a short time in South Boston, where he made the acquaintance of Dr. W. T. Parker, who introduced him to the dissecting-room in Mason Street, Boston. During this time he painted several pictures upon religious subjects for Father Fitz Simmons of South Boston, some of which were afterward burned with the Catholic church, the rest having been sent to churches in the country. He also painted at this time a picture of THE INFANT SAVIOUR, which he afterward gave to a Catholic fair in Boston. For a number of years it was at the Orphans' Home, on Shawmut Avenue, where Dr. Rimmer saw it while Sister Alexis was in charge of that institution; but it has now disappeared.

The earliest picture by her husband, of which Mrs. Rimmer has any remembrance, was called THE SNUFF-TAKER. It was painted on wood, and afterward destroyed by the artist himself.

# CHAPTER IV.

### RANDOLPH.

#### 1845-1855.

IN 1845 Dr. Rimmer settled in Randolph, and began to practise the trade of a shoemaker as his chief occupation. Of this course he writes : —

"For a while matters went on well enough ; but the business of portrait-painting, notwithstanding all my exertions, failed to yield sufficient income. Every one, at some time, in these regions, worked at shoe-making. Boys left the shoe-shop to enter college, to work in stores, and to learn other trades : so I too, as I had commenced the study of medicine, took to shoe-making. It implied no loss of respectability. Thirty-five years ago, all those who were most respectable were once in the shoe-business as journeymen ; but, even had it been otherwise, it would have been the same to me. I was without friends whom I would have permitted to assist me : my family had to be supported, and I was thankful for the opportunity of earning my living at an honest calling."

In Randolph, as it had been elsewhere, the Catholic priest was the ready patron and appreciative friend of the artist. Father Roddan invited him to play the organ, and conduct the music of the church, as well as to instruct the children of the parish in music, — duties which Dr. Rimmer performed for a number of years. He also painted for Father Roddan a large altar-piece, containing the figures of the Virgin, the Infant Jesus, and Joseph, all life-size, and two smaller pictures. The latter I was fortunate enough to find, although they had been removed from their places more than twenty years before. One of them, THE CRUCIFIXION, was painted without a model, and in a barn. The color is not particularly interesting, but the picture shows considerable knowledge of the human figure. The other, THE INFANT ST. PETER, was painted from the artist's little son, and is a curious composition. Dr. Rimmer evidently felt the delicate, tender color, form, and flesh of infancy; but with thirty years of mellowing the tone is yet a trifle warm.

Every moment the doctor could get during his ten-years' residence in Randolph, aside from the time given to his trade and studies, he spent in painting portraits, ideal compositions, and miniatures. Neither did he wholly relinquish sculpture; for he cut a small portrait bust of his oldest daughter, then three years old, in marble. He worked sitting upon the floor, and holding the block between his knees, illustrating in the process a cardinal principle of his nature and teachings. He believed in using models, and studying life to gain knowledge and a great power of expression; in the execution of a work rarely consulting the model, but depending entirely upon his memory and imagination. In executing this bust, he relied upon the glimpses he caught as his daughter passed him in the room, as reminders of his memory. The same work also illustrated another element of his artistic nature. He sought to go directly to the result without any preliminary steps, such as first making a model in clay, casting it in plaster, and then learning the use of tools. The face and neck of this bust are beautifully executed. There was not quite enough marble on one side of the head to make the ear, and the sculptor fitted in a piece with the utmost precision.

Many of the portraits at Randolph were destroyed, simply from having become uninteresting to the owners; and those now to be found are for the most part wholly unimportant except as being the work of Dr. Rimmer. I have seen, however, one miniature, executed at this time, exquisitely delicate in drawing and tender in color. The artist occasionally sold a picture for from ten to twenty dollars in Boston, in some auction; and he had occasional commissions to add cattle, or some other accessory, to a landscape, for which quickly executed task he received usually two or three dollars. I was fortunate enough to discover one of these twenty-dollar pictures. Its sole merits were great distance and solid construction.

While at Randolph, Dr. Rimmer worked with such intense zeal at his various occupations that he more than once fell from his shoemaking bench from sheer exhaustion. He earned enough to buy a small home, which, however, he soon sold, loaning to a needy friend the money received. Here, as elsewhere, his life was made up of extremes of happiness and sorrow. A family of boys and girls was growing up about him; and he longed for a more even future for himself and

14. CRUCIFIXION

13. INFANT ST. PETER

them. But suddenly the hand of death was laid upon three of his boys, and hope went out in mourning.

During his ten-years' residence in Randolph, his relations with people about him were much as they always had been, and as they continued until his death. Indeed, out of his family circle, he had in his whole life only three confidential friends, — Mr. Daniel Howard of Randolph; Mr. Andrew Bradshaw of Brooklyn, N.Y.; and Col. C. A. Nichols of Providence, R.I.

The following is Mr. Howard's estimate of his friend: —

"I have known Dr. Rimmer intimately since 1848. He was by nature the best, truest, and ablest man I ever met. He possessed the nicest sense of honor, and the qualities which distinguish superior minds. It was always a great delight to me to hear him talk, and we have spent many nights conversing. Common people said he 'talked in the clouds;' but the masses repelled him, and he was with most men reserved and repellant. He regretted this, but was not able to help it. He was extremely sensitive to spiritual influences, and often advanced ideas upon this subject as beautiful as they were startling. I believe he thought more about the unseen world than of the one in which he lived. His perception was wonderfully accurate. I remember an instance where his advice in a business matter was strange, and apparently absurd; but I had such confidence in his foresight that I followed it against my own judgment, with a result favorable to myself, as he had predicted.

"Rimmer was a prominent member of our debating society, and was always deferred to in matters where a wide acquaintance with books was necessary for a just decision. Mr. O. A. Brownson came here to lecture on Catholicism; and after the lecture, as usual in country towns, a crowd collected in the bar-room of the hotel to talk the matter over. Brownson and Rimmer were soon engaged in a warm discussion, and we thought Rimmer had the best of the argument. After he went out, Brownson asked who that man was, and was told that he was a shoemaker. 'And,' said Brownson, 'a remarkable man. He has read, but not studied.'

"I think Rimmer cured his patients with his hands and sympathy, rather than with medicine. He should be judged by a high standard. I sometimes think that the faults of such men are real virtues when rightly regarded. I never knew any thing about his origin; and he never referred to it but once, when he said, 'You would be the most surprised man in Randolph if I should tell you who I really am; and I will tell you some day.' He was out of his element here in Randolph, and, I think, out of it in this country. He ought to have lived among the greatest men in the world, where definite and progressive results were the tests, where the bitterest antagonisms bring out the highest and truest mettle. I don't care so much what a man is, as what he might be under fair circumstances. He had the most wonderful possibilities. What he accomplished is one proof of that; but a better proof to me was my own appreciation of the interior of his real nature. The existence of such a person in New England, under our Puritan influences, is one of those phenomena for which there is no explanation. He was not what is called a cultured man, and I doubt if cultured people would like him. The conventionality and hypocrisy of the world he hated beyond measure. Against the wrongs of unjust laws, the sufferings of the poor, and the inequalities of justice, he could not hold his peace."

While Dr. Rimmer was spending ten of the best years of his life on the shoe-maker's bench in a little country village, the artist who was a few years later to be his principal contemporary, and a living element in Boston art for nearly twenty years, was enjoying the friendship and acquaintance of the strongest minds which adorned his profession in the world, studying with the best masters of the time in the art-centre of the world, and making himself familiar with the art-treasures of the centuries. No sharper contrast could be imagined than that presented between the lives of William Rimmer and William Morris Hunt; the former living in the withering sterility of a New-England village, the latter feasting upon the study of Italian, Dutch, French, and Spanish art. To Rimmer every thing was denied except genius: to Hunt every thing was given that his ardent and demanding nature required. Rimmer lived and studied in worse than solitude, for he constantly felt the burden of an unsympathetic world. He shunned men, and knew neither art nor artists. He stood alone, proud, inflexible, and often disdainful. Hunt drank at every refreshing, golden source, and was affected by every glorious, reviving art-influence. He felt the necessity of new life, new men, and new inspiration, and had a mind strong enough for constant progress, even under the most discouraging circumstances. He was a great finder and a great doer. When Hunt was in admiring association with Lessing, Barye, Millet, Daumier, Diaz, Couture, Rousseau, and other giants of modern art, Rimmer was working like a slave, striving to feed and comfort a feeble wife and a growing young family, in an out-of-the-way village, where there was but one soul outside his doors with whom he could claim and receive a frank and loving confidence. Such were the conditions under which he was enlarging his powerful imagination, and thinking out art-problems common to none but the great artists who have lived under the most beneficent patronage, in ages when art had its dignities, and received the acknowledgment of its divine existence without question or argument. Hunt set on fire every art-nature that he met, and took from it the very fire he kindled. He was the first and best-educated artist of his country; and no artist of his time was more ripe in the intelligence, purpose, and nature of art, or had a more subtle conception of what art is.

Rimmer was the first artist on this continent who had a thorough art-knowledge and understanding of the human figure in its single and composite character.

His charm is in the imagination, and his work appeals to another generation. Had Rimmer possessed half of Hunt's worldly wisdom, there is nothing that he could not have accomplished.

# CHAPTER V.

## EAST MILTON.

### 1855-1861.

URING the last years of his stay at Randolph, Dr. Rimmer began to practise medicine as occasion offered. In 1855, after a fruitless prospecting visit to Lowell, he removed his family to Chelsea, Mass., where he began systematically the practice of his new profession. A distinguished specialist from Boston, whom he called in for consultation in a difficult case, finding Rimmer practising with neither professional examination nor diploma, and being pleased with his treatment of the patient, advised him to join the Suffolk County Medical Society; which the doctor did, receiving a diploma.

While in Chelsea, Dr. Rimmer lost one of his two remaining sons.

Before the close of the year 1855, finding that his prospects were not what he wished, he left this place, and removed to East Milton, a small hamlet in the town of Milton, and not far from Quincy. Twenty-five years ago East Milton contained few inhabitants, mostly workmen employed in the quarries, — a class not too plentifully endowed with sensibility. Slight indeed must have been the encouragement for a physician in such a locality; and inspiring human relations were utterly wanting. Was it his extreme sensitiveness that led Dr. Rimmer into such a place? his sympathy for the poor that made him go where others would not? or was it that unseen and often unrecognized guide that conducts men in the mysterious way of destiny? It was a hard fate which led him into such unsympathetic surroundings, and into the very face of mountains of granite, that repulsive, self-protective material, which, for the first time on this continent, was to find in him a conqueror, and out of which he was to carve his signature as the most powerful genius in sculpture that has yet appeared in this country.

24

The experience which was inevitable to Dr. Rimmer came to pass in Milton no less than elsewhere. Qualities are necessary to the popularity of a physician which he did not possess, and without these profound knowledge is not sufficient. He was successful in several difficult cases, being especially distinguished in treating typhoid-fever; but it soon became evident that his practice would not support his family. He went much among the sick or wounded quarrymen, and his kindness and tenderness with the poor were unbounded. No more appreciative or beautiful tribute to his sympathy and benevolence to the unfortunate could be imagined than that paid to him by some of his patients twenty-five years after. "No man," says one of them, "ever entered a sick-room with such delicacy and kindness. He seemed to regard himself as responsible for the lives of those he attended, and he shrank from no sacrifices in their behalf. He suffered scarcely less than those to whom he ministered; and no inclemencies of weather, or his own extreme bodily fatigue, prevented his frequent visits, not only in the capacity of a physician, but as a kind friend, carrying to the sick some delicacy from his own scanty store. Several times he saved the lives of persons given up by other doctors, because he gave remedies and performed operations which they dared not. I do not know what he was as an artist; but nothing could equal his devotion to the poor and suffering, though his return was too often abuse and insult."

Dr. Rimmer's endurance of physical pain was as great as his courage. Twice, while driving in the night, he was thrown from his buggy, breaking his nose each time; and on each occasion he attended to his duties before returning home, then setting the broken bone himself.

Death followed him to Milton, and here he buried his only remaining son. This blow was one of the most cruel he ever experienced. From the time when in boyhood he learned from his father the story of the latter's origin, he had cherished the hope that some time favoring fortune would bring to him and to his the inheritance of name and wealth which should belong to the eldest son of Thomas Rimmer. The birth of his own sons he interpreted as assurances that time would unravel the knot of fate, and his cherished ambitions be at last fulfilled. With the death of his last boy died also the hope of glories which must depend upon the perpetuation of the male line; and nothing but persistent bravery, and affection for his wife and three surviving daughters, prevented his sinking into effortless despair.

Finding his practice insufficient to support him, Dr. Rimmer conceived the idea of eking out his narrow income by working in granite. His power of production in form had been unexercised for many years, but during that time his knowledge of the human figure had greatly increased. He procured a shapeless piece of granite, and began to fashion it into the likeness of a human head. It was the action of desperation upon a no less desperate material.

While thus engaged he was called to attend a patient, who thus relates his experience and intercourse with the doctor : —

" I came in personal contact with Dr. Rimmer, for the first time, in 1858, when I called him to treat me for bronchitis. I saw that he was not a common man. He cured me ; and I offered him a hundred dollars, — not because I owed him as much, or that I thought he would accept that sum for his services, but because I wanted him to have the money. He refused the money ; but I persuaded him to accept it by asking him to take charge of my family whenever they were sick. The doctor was very poor, — had little practice. He was too shy, and could not push himself. I happened to be the first man in town to see that he was entitled to a much greater consideration than he received. He was a delightful man to meet, — tender, sensitive, pleasing, and intelligent. The best people whom he knew appreciated him. He was arrested for debt by a Braintree butcher. The bill amounted to seventy-five or a hundred dollars. I paid it ; and, to cancel the amount, Rimmer cut a granite head for a building on the corner of Franklin and Devonshire Streets, Boston. The building was burned in the great fire. I was in the granite business at the time. I gave him the granite out of which he cut the female head and the St. Stephen. I believed that if Dr. Rimmer could only have a chance he would do great things ; and I knew of no one who would be more likely to be interested in him than Mr. Stephen H. Perkins, — a noble, generous-hearted man, who lived in Milton, and whom I had known since 1831. I spoke to Rimmer about Perkins, but he expressed his aversion to taking any steps to make Perkins's acquaintance, and Perkins would not believe what I told him concerning the doctor ; but finally I managed to get them together at my house. Perkins soon called at the doctor's, saw his work in granite, and listened to his demonstrations in drawing and explanations of the construction of the human figure. It surprised Perkins, and aroused his enthusiasm. From that moment their friendship began, and continued without ceasing. I remember that Rimmer had such a fear of meeting people that he said to me, when I spoke of Perkins, ' I won't be trotted out. I like to meet people, but I won't run after them. Some people are like ashes in my eyes.' He was fond of theatricals, and trained the pupils of a school in West Quincy to play ' Still Waters Run Deep.' He gave me one of his pictures. Was always grateful for any kindness. Once said to me, ' If ever I reach the topmost round of the ladder of fame, I want to thank you for putting my foot on the first round.' As soon as the head for the Devonshire-street building was completed, the doctor began another, — a more pretentious task, of a piece of decoration, also in granite. To assist in hewing off the rough, and working down to the general form, the doctor hired a workman, who charged for his labor almost as much as the sum the doctor was to receive for the finished work. This experience was not encouraging, and he henceforth did all the work himself. His next work was a female head, life-size, cut with much delicacy and fine modelling."

Concerning a certain class of people with whom he was brought in contact, Dr. Rimmer writes in his diary : —

" I cannot conceive of any thing in the human form more brutish than one of these big, raw-boned, illiterate, uncultivated Vermont and New-Hampshire boors. Selfishness, unmitigated selfishness, and a complete disregard of every thing sacred ; a want of every honorable, noble, or generous impulse ; together with the absence of every tender sensibility, — save in what concerns themselves, — seem to distinguish them from all other men. Keenly alive to every thing that concerns themselves, their interests, feelings, or schemes, they speak and act, when appealing to others, like men ; but in relation to others — their wants, interests, or feelings — they are as destitute of any human or honorable sentiment as wolves. They talk of virtue, that their rights may be respected ; of humanity, that they may not be injured ; of kindness, that they may be well used ; of sympathy, that they may be befriended ; of honesty, that they may get their own ; of forbearance, that they may escape punishment : while in their dealings with others they are heartless, overreaching, cunning, unscrupulous practisers of every thing that is unmanly, dishonest, and contemptible ; and to appeal to their honor or feelings is but to subject one's self to greater outrage and deeper insult."

Writing of his poor health, the cheerless resort of granite-cutting, and the physical pain that he endured, he says : —

" But what better am I than other men in this hard world, where Nature holds dominion, and Nature alone, — where the cold wind has no mercy, the storm no feeling ; where all the elements do their will, and all the powers move at pleasure ? We are but mites who live in spite of forces that do their spite as they are moved, as they must do at all times. What better am I than others, who as atoms crawl by the force that is in them beneath the clouds, in sunshine and rain, heat and cold, upon this damp crust ? that crawl about or dig, like other mites, to protect themselves against the inclemencies of nature? What better? What am I but one of these vermin? I believe in the existence of a spirit-world, and of immortality; but what good does that do us? Has this fact saved us any pain, clothed, fed, or cared for us, either now or in past days?"

# CHAPTER VI.

## EAST MILTON.

### 1855-1861.

M R. STEPHEN H. PERKINS became Dr. Rimmer's good angel, and was the only man with whom the latter had in his art-life uninterrupted friendly and business relations. Mr. Perkins encouraged his friend to continue his efforts as a sculptor.

"Be an artist," he said: "there are plenty of doctors, but few artists."

As a response to this friendly interest was executed the St. Stephen. It was cut from a block of granite, and, as in the case of his previous work in sculpture, without a model or any of the facilities usually considered indispensable for the accomplishment of such an undertaking. It represents the head of a man past middle age, in great agony, thrown upward and back, as if vainly appealing for protection, while the raised right shoulder indicates the arm lifted in defence. It might almost be said that the work symbolizes Dr. Rimmer's relation to the world. It shows combative, wonderful, concentrative haste, and is a striking illustration of the characteristics of his nature.

The artist's habit of working without preliminary sketches arose from his impetuous, dominating nature. It was not from the lack of appreciation of the value of routine preparation and of technical knowledge. His long and careful study of anatomy had given him a thorough knowledge of the construction of the human body; but he had not patience to prepare a model, or even a sketch of his work. His emotion neither reasoned, nor waited for preliminaries. He worked with such desperate rage in hewing from its obdurate material the head of St. Stephen, that his hands were blistered and torn, his arms swollen, and his whole body exhausted in aching sympathy with the activity of his spirit.

The head was completed in the space of four weeks, in the latter part of 1860. Early in December of that year it was placed on exhibition in the art-gallery of Williams and Everett. The following letter in regard to it appeared in " The Boston Evening Journal" of Dec. 10, 1860, and is interesting as being, so far as is known, the first public notice of the work of Dr. Rimmer.

### HEAD OF ST. STEPHEN.

*To the Editor of " The Boston Journal."*

Sir, — Will you allow me, in brief space, to call the attention of all persons interested in art to a remarkable piece of sculpture in granite, now to be seen at Williams & Everett's? It is by Dr. Rimmer, a practising physician at Quincy, and was cut by him directly from the block, without any previous modelling in clay, or even drawing. Of course these circumstances, and the stubbornness of the material, add nothing to the artistic value of the work; but they are important to our estimate of the artist, as showing the definiteness and completeness of conception that alone could give an unpractised hand such mastery over a material allowing no revision, and in which the mere technical difficulties must absorb so much attention.

The same masterly power, seeing its subject in all its parts at a glance, is shown in the harmony of the composition, and in the treatment of the surface.

The work of a novice, however studiously wrought, is betrayed by a stiffness and dryness that come from an elaboration of parts, without a constant feeling of the whole, and from an uncertainty about the surface. It has no *movement*, as the French say, because there is no concert among the members, however accurate in themselves. The power above insisted on is doubtless the highest technical merit that a sculptor can possess; and, if I am not mistaken in attributing a large share of it to Dr. Rimmer, it shows that he already occupies a high position in the art. This work is incidentally valuable as showing what can be done with granite, which, if we are to have out-of-door sculpture, is our only fit material. I understand it was used by Dr. Rimmer, rather to test the capacity of the stone, and that he does not consider it so suitable as marble for ordinary subjects, though he thinks it eminently proper for a statue meant to stand in the open air, and of size sufficient to overpower the obtrusiveness of the grain, — the very quality of the opacity that spoils it for close view giving it greater distinctness and depth to the shadows.                                                           C.

The St. Stephen is the most complete work of sculpture that its author executed. In respect to the material, it was the most difficult in its execution: it is thoroughly well constructed, well understood, and executed with an accomplished sense of expressional effect. Its detailed forms, the arrangement of its masses.

16. HEAD IN GRANITE

15. ST. STEPHEN

its solidity and grasp, are as profound and forcible as the circumstances of its existence are wonderful.

Mr. Perkins, who had been deeply impressed with Dr. Rimmer's powers, especially when taken in connection with the fact that the latter had received no art instruction save that which his father had given him, and who had talked much in Boston of the Milton physician as "another Michael Angelo," was triumphant and delighted by the flattering reception which the bust met with in the city. He desired strongly that the work might find a purchaser, although its author had small hope of such good fortune. Dr. Rimmer had not even gone so far as to estimate its value. "When asked by Mr. Perkins and Col. E. C. Cabot," to quote the words of one who knew the circumstances, "how much he thought it worth, he began to count its actual cost by reckoning so much for tool-sharpening, so many hours' work, and so on. Before he had completed this process of cost-counting, they cut him short by declaring its value to be at least five hundred dollars. On hearing this sum, to him so enormous, Rimmer looked as though the earth had opened at his feet."

The bust did not, however, find a purchaser, — a fact which Mr. Perkins explained by remarking that "it is necessary that a work of art have a distinguished origin in order to give it a money value to the majority of people." This gentleman was in no way discouraged by the absence of any pecuniary result in the exhibition of the St. Stephen; for he strongly encouraged the doctor to execute a full-sized statue, giving beautiful evidence of his sincerity, as is proved by the record in Dr. Rimmer's diary: "Jan. 27, 1861, received of Mr. Perkins a hundred dollars, with which to begin the statue of the Falling Gladiator."

On the 4th of the following month this important work was begun. It was executed without the assistance of models, except such aid as the sculptor could derive from the study of his own body, in two hundred hours stolen from days already fully occupied in the arduous and poorly paid duties of his profession; being completed on the 10th of June, 1861, in the sculptor's forty-sixth year.

The sculptor worked in a small, low-windowed basement-room of the house in which he lived. The lower half of the window was covered, so that passers-by could not observe what was going on within, the house being almost on the line of the sidewalk. He worked without any of the facilities usually employed by sculptors for the setting-up of a statue in clay, bracing up with sticks the different parts as he built them with his hands. The difficulties he encountered were innumerable. He had no fire in the room. The clay froze and dried, cracking and falling down, so that parts of the statue were made many times over. As it neared completion, it became more difficult than ever to keep the figure from total destruction; and it was finally cast in plaster, and finished in that material. The workmen who performed this operation came near destroying the entire statue; and to their carelessness they added the charge of what Dr. Rimmer understood to be an extravagant price for their labor. Of this last complication the artist writes: "Such is the pressure of life everywhere, in all men, that truth is of less importance than gain, the soul less than the body."

Properly speaking, Dr. Rimmer was not a modeller: he did not develop a statue by a general and gradual building-up, either in an anatomical or constructive sense; but he piled up the clay or plaster, and cut from it the figure, after the manner of a wood or stone carver. Hard and continuous study from life he neither practised nor taught, differing in this respect from the best sculptors the world over. He worked from the outside in, not from the inside out, as far, at least, as material was concerned. He became satisfied, even before the completion of the GLADIATOR, that he needed experience in the mechanical contrivances for setting up a figure in clay; but he seems never to have changed materially his method of working.

During the execution of the GLADIATOR, Mr. Perkins watched its daily progress with the liveliest interest. Professor W. R. Ware, Col. E. C. Cabot, and many other citizens of Boston, who were interested in art, also visited the sculptor during its execution, and expressed their warmest solicitude for its success. Mr. Perkins was so anxious that it should be perfect, that he criticised it with full and friendly freedom. The doctor listened to all his suggestions, and was desirous of testing their value to please his friend, although many of the criticisms of Mr. Perkins caused additional and useless labor. Dr. Rimmer says in his diary: "Was visited by Mr. Perkins on Wednesday. From a remark made by him I was induced to alter the foot: in consequence, I had to alter the whole leg without effecting any thing, — making matters worse at every stroke."

The way in which Dr. Rimmer received the numerous visitors whom the growing interest in his work brought to Milton, may be judged from the following account of a visit given by one of them: —

"After rapping several times at the door, it was at last partly opened, and the head of a man appeared, while an important and rather gruff voice asked, 'What do you want?' I answered that I was looking for Dr. Rimmer, who I had learned was making some interesting works of sculpture, and that I wished to see them. 'Dr. Rimmer is not on exhibition, neither is his house a museum,' replied the head, which I supposed was the doctor's. I added that I was a friend of Mr. Perkins, and through his invitation had come from Boston on purpose to see the sculptor and his work; that I was interested in art, and felt a friendly interest in artists, and did not wish to be disappointed in the object of my journey.

" After some hesitation on the part of the sculptor, I was admitted, — no doubt solely out of consideration for Mr. Perkins, — and saw the statue of the FALLING GLADIATOR. We were on good terms in a short time. The doctor's interest in and knowledge of art were soon manifested by a number of drawings that he made with chalk on the wall of the room. I had never seen any thing like it, and I could not understand or explain the existence of such a person. We had never had such an artist in Boston. Every one who cared a fig for art became interested in Rimmer; and it was determined to induce him to come to the city, and give instruction."

Mr. Perkins had had the ST. STEPHEN photographed, selling the pictures at five dollars each, to procure money to pay the bill for casting in plaster the GLADIATOR. As soon as this cast was completed, he had it also photographed, disposing of copies among his friends in Boston for the sculptor.

Taking into consideration the circumstances of its production, the FALLING GLADIATOR is certainly a prodigious work. It is thoroughly conceived and composed: it shows a profound sense of the construction, movement, weight, and balance of the human figure. Portions of the statue are as well done as they could be under the most favorable circumstances. Especially remarkable are the action and folds of flesh on the left side, the lines of the abdomen, breast, and back. The work lacks the nervous touch, the freshness and clearness of form, which distinguish the finest statues. The French or Italian sense of nature is not predominant in any of Dr. Rimmer's work. With him every thing was subordinated to the exemplification of an idea or a principle.

The FALLING GLADIATOR is undoubtedly the most remarkable work of sculpture that has yet been produced in this country. It is powerful, wonderful, but not alluring. There are those who have considered it simply a study of anatomy; but it is a contribution to the sculpture of America, produced without indebtedness to her institutions or her sympathies. It is a sad evidence of conditions which ought not to exist. That such a work could be tossed about in plaster for twenty years, and finally be forgotten, is in itself a terribly severe reflection upon our pretended fondness for antique sculpture. We can only love and appreciate the antique in proportion as we understand and foster our own productions.

Were sculpture recognized in this country as a necessity, the FALLING GLADIATOR would long ago have been reproduced in bronze, and erected in some locality worthy of sculptured honor.

# CHAPTER VII.

## EAST MILTON.

### 1855-1861.

URING these years in East Milton, Dr. Rimmer painted several pictures. An interesting incident connected with one of these is related by a physician who knew him at this time.

"I first became acquainted with Dr. Rimmer," this gentleman writes, "by being called to consult with him in a case of typhoid-fever, a disease in the treatment of which he was very successful. There was a rumor that he was practising without a diploma; and certain members of the county medical society were angry at my repeated consultations with him, threatening to bring the matter up at our annual meeting. I said nothing, merely making up my mind, that, if this were done, I should tell them that I thought brains better than diplomas, and that I much preferred consulting with the former; but the matter never went beyond threats. One winter morning I met Dr. Rimmer trudging up the hill with a bundle under his arm. 'I am going to your house,' he said, 'with a testimony of my gratitude to you for your kindness.' The bundle contained an oil painting; and this expression of gratitude, which I believe to have been genuine, is to me priceless. I took the picture to a Boston art-dealer to procure a frame. 'Ah!' he said, 'a foreign painting, I see.' — 'No,' I answered: 'it is the work of a poor country physician.' His interest vanished at once, and he began immediately to discover faults in it."

I have found two of the pictures painted in East Milton, — the MASSACRE OF THE INNOCENTS, and HAGAR AND ISHMAEL. The former is owned by Dr. Holmes of Milton, and the latter by Mr. George Penniman of Boston. The former is the first of Dr. Rimmer's pictures that I have seen which shows the artist's unusual power of composition, as afterward so abundantly expressed in his drawings and other pictorial work. The painting represents a woman sitting on the roof of a temple situated upon a height that overlooks a vast plain. She leans against an altar upon which incense is burning. The nude child, half-lying in her lap, is beautifully painted, and understood in a large way. Both figures are quite unconscious of danger, the child holding out his hand playfully to some object which has attracted his attention. Suddenly and unperceived a villain approaches from behind, grasping the mother by the wrist of that arm which could, if free, protect her child, and preparing to plunge his knife, terrible in shape, into the child. Far down on the plain are seen other mothers contending with murderers for the lives of their innocent ones. The idea that the artist wished to convey seems to have been, that this mother had gone to the top of the temple, where incense to the gods was burning, there placing herself and child under its divinely perfumed and most sacred guardianship with perfect confidence in its protective potency. To find human cruelty triumphant in such a place, and Heaven merciless, overcomes her; and she turns her eyes upward in an agony of protesting, despairing appeal. The light of the picture centres upon the child, the figures of the woman and the murderer being mannered and uninteresting.

The HAGAR AND ISHMAEL is composed with the central idea of accenting the grief of the mother, whose figure nearly fills the entire canvas. The color is very bad.

It may be as well to follow out here the fate of the FALLING GLADIATOR, since this work properly belongs to the history of the artist's life at East Milton. In 1862 Mr. Perkins sailed for Europe, taking with him, by Dr. Rimmer's consent, plaster copies of this statue and of the ST. STEPHEN. The casts were first exhibited in London, and afterward in the Paris *Salon* of 1863. The GLADIATOR was declared, by certain persons who saw it in the latter city, to be a cast from life, and the attempt to palm it off as a modelled statue ridiculed. The story is too absurd for consideration, for no artist of any sense would ever have dreamed of such an idea. Mr. Perkins, with all his kindly zeal, was ignorant of the way in which such matters should be conducted in Paris, and unfortunately fell into the hands of M. Louisone, who was any thing but the proper person to introduce such a work in Parisian art circles. It is not known whether the casts were seen by any of the distinguished French artists capable of appreciating such works, but they at least were admired by several well-known critics.

17.   THE FALLING GLADIATOR

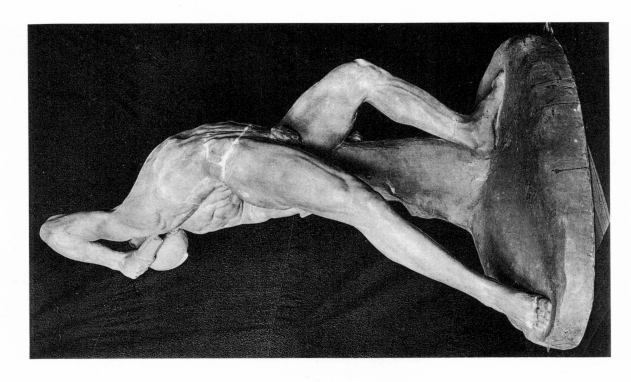

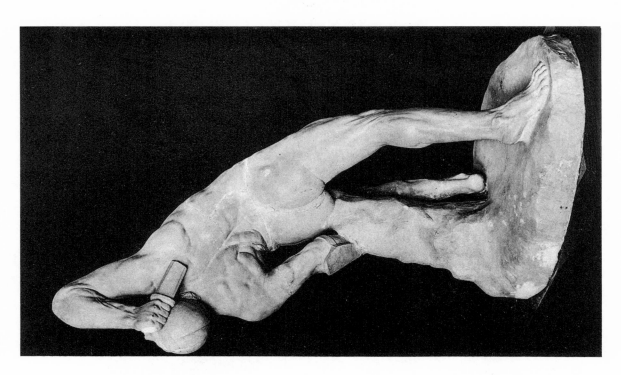

18. The Falling Gladiator

Later in the same year Mr. Perkins took the casts to Florence, where they were seen by Dupré, one of the oldest of modern Italian sculptors, who expressed his gratification at seeing them, sending to Dr. Rimmer the encouraging message, " By all means, keep on." Other sculptors pronounced the GLADIATOR a " miracle of art," although they were incredulous of the statement that it was made without the use of a living model.

The cast of the ST. STEPHEN was sent to Berlin at the solicitation of one of its admirers, to be deposited in the National Gallery of Plaster Casts. The GLADIATOR remained in Florence until within a few years, when it was destroyed.

Mr. Perkins had hoped, that, by taking these casts to Europe, he might win for his friend a recognition abroad which would greatly improve the artist's standing at home. These good intentions came to nought. In a true sense, it was unjust to Dr. Rimmer to bring his work into comparison and competition with the productions of foreign artists. This haste to attract foreign attention is one of the besetting sins of Americans, and evinces a want of patience and self-respect. It was illogical to bring the GLADIATOR into competition with works of sculptors who had enjoyed the best opportunities of study. The conditions of production were vastly unequal, yet in the consideration of the works this fact was necessarily lost sight of. Dr. Rimmer consented to the exhibition in the hope that his works might be seen by those capable of appreciating them, and who would understand the difficulties surrounding an artist in this country.

The reception of Dr. Rimmer's productions in Europe did not for an instant shake the hearty faith and friendship of Mr. Perkins. He wrote to the artist from Florence, urging the latter to execute some sculpture for exhibition in Paris in 1867, and offering to take charge of its reproduction in marble in Italy. He also endeavored to arrange that the sculptor should go to Florence for a term of years, being persuaded that with the facilities afforded by that city, he would·succeed in a manner which should confer honor both upon himself and his country. Dr. Rimmer fully appreciated Mr. Perkins, and regarded his friendship as the most pleasing event of his life. He often attended him as a physician, and enjoyed the hospitality of his home, such a friend being immeasurably dearer from the fact that the artist's peculiar temper and sensitive nature made it nearly impossible for ordinary men long to continue friendly relations with him.

The original plaster cast of the GLADIATOR was exhibited in Boston on various occasions for several years before Dr. Rimmer moved to New York. It was also shown at the exhibition of the National Academy of Design in 1865 or 1866, and was afterward removed to the Cooper Institute when Dr. Rimmer assumed the charge of the School of Design in that institution. A few years after he left, it was placed in a storeroom with articles not needed for daily use. In the spring of 1880, it was sent to the Boston Museum of Fine Arts, where it now occupies an honored position.

No pecuniary return came to the sculptor for the GLADIATOR. The ST. STEPHEN, after having been exhibited in Boston and New York, was purchased by Mr. Perkins for one hundred and fifty dollars, and by him presented to the Boston Athenæum. Neither work has had any perceptible effect upon the sculpture of the country; although it is just to say, that, up to this time, no work of sculpture, however meritorious, would make itself perceptibly felt here. There is an admiration for sculpture and for what is called such; but a sensitive understanding and positive love for its existence, or demand for its production, does not yet exist.

It has been observed in regard to Dr. Rimmer's work as a whole: " It is neither inspiring nor fructifying in its nature: it produces no abiding impression upon the mind. Powerful and imaginative in itself, it yet was not vital in him as coming from a source of constant and absolute expression, or to others as a suggestive, impellant activity. His art had no youth. It was born in full manhood, — self-taught, solitary, imperious, and uneven. It was subordinate to his domestic nature, a capacity for himself; it was employed as occasion required, not a message or prophecy: wonderful to an extraordinary degree when the circumstances surrounding its production are remembered, but not human enough to permanently touch the sympathies."

But this judgment ignores the fact that there is no art constituency in this country; and it is therefore too severe.

## CHAPTER VIII.

### BOSTON.

### 1861–1866.

THE most important result of the production of the St. Stephen and the Gladiator was the interest which these works excited in Boston, and which led to the sculptor's being invited to the city to give lectures and instruction in art anatomy. Col. E. C. Cabot, Professor W. R. Ware, Mr. S. H. Perkins, and other prominent gentlemen, united cordially in this invitation; yet Dr. Rimmer considered it with much hesitancy and misgiving. He was closely wedded to his domestic life, and dreaded exchanging the pleasures of home for the to him painful ordeal of a public stage; while he furthermore doubted the ultimate value of lectures as a sufficient means of art education. His health was far from good, he having suffered for many years from palpitation of the heart; and he feared the effect of excitement and fatigue. The welfare of his family being, however, his principal thought, he accepted the invitation; though he observed to a friend, "I am through with the world, and I feel that the best thing for me to do is to help on a proper school, — to start the idea of art education in the right way. That is a great deal."

On Nov. 1, 1861, Dr. Rimmer began his lectures in room No. 55 of Studio Building. They were attended by old and young of all classes and both sexes, — by artists who wished to learn, by literary people who came to enjoy an intellectual feast, and by physicians and other professionals who were delighted to see the human figure delineated and its art functions explained. No man had ever appeared in Boston who exhibited such knowledge, such facility in drawing every part of the figure, both in its details and in its composite character. It was the first living element in art instruction Boston had ever possessed.

Dr. Rimmer's reception and prospects were very flattering. His method of teaching was new, and would be so to-day. He drew in chalk upon a blackboard every bone and muscle with which the artist needed to be acquainted; first as an independent fact, and then in its relations to the formation of the complete figure. Each member of the body was next drawn, to illustrate its principal physical movements, actions, and purposes; and finally the entire figure was similarly illustrated.

Every emotion, every passion, every instinct, and every intellectual operation of the mind, as manifested through the form and features, were portrayed in the minutest particulars. The various types of mankind, through all their phases of progress or retrogression, were illustrated and compared. "Often through the lectures," remarks one who heard them, " he would speak of the characteristics of the different races, not only as a student familiar with books, but as a man who by intuitive sequence understood the principles upon which the races were developed."

The drawings were made, moreover, not only as illustrative of facts, as is usually the case in works on art anatomy, but every figure was a complete composition, or drawn — with reference to its use — as a component part of a composition of several figures. Dr. Rimmer accompanied the drawings with exhaustive oral explanations. As soon as an object was drawn on the blackboard, the pupil was expected to copy it in his sketch-book, writing down the observations made in relation to it. While this was being done, the doctor went about among the pupils, giving hints and explanations. As soon as the pupil had attained proficiency, he was required to sketch upon the blackboard the exercises previously studied, to be criticised by the master and other pupils. The delineations were followed by the use of the skeleton and living models, Dr. Rimmer often taking from the audience some person as an illustration of the type of character under consideration.

So far as delineation and explanation could answer in a system of art education, this method was as comprehensive as any that could well be imagined. Its value to the student depended upon his capacity to retain in memory what he was taught, and upon his quickness in transferring drawings and observations to his note-book. For the acquisition of general artistic knowledge of the human figure, it was undoubtedly the best method: as productive of individual results, it was the teaching of the lecture-room, and not the seriously discovered and applied knowledge of the progressive student. It seemed to be precisely what was needed by the persons who attended the lectures. Many artists were always present; and their note-books attest the completeness of Dr. Rimmer's understanding of the subject, as well as their own earnestness and talent.

Perhaps the most important element in this art instruction was, that it came through the inspiring medium of a strong man. Once touched by the charm of expressing his long-accumulating knowledge, Dr. Rimmer became inspired; and the study of anatomical forms, which had hitherto been dry and irksome, became, under his lucid descriptions, electric presence, and skilful hand, an enchanting pursuit.

From Milton to Boston was a great change for the artist. For the first time he met the interests, minds, and activities of the art-centre of America. His fears in regard to public speaking proved but too well founded: to appear before an audience cost him a severe mental and physical strain. Profuse perspiration testified to his extreme agitation; and it may be said that every stroke upon the blackboard cost him so much life. Often after a drawing was made he was forced to retire while the pupils were copying it, in order to gain breath and strength to continue his lecture.

The interest in the lecturer and his work increased rapidly; and a petition was sent to the authorities of the Lowell Institute, asking that Dr. Rimmer should be invited to give a course of lectures there. The petition was favorably received, and the course begun Oct. 14, 1863. The hall was so crowded at these lectures that he delivered an extra series in the afternoon for ladies, that the regular evenings might be given up, to gentlemen exclusively. At his suggestion a class was formed, including most of the artists, draughtsmen, and architects in Boston, for the purpose of drawing from casts at the Boston Athenæum, the doctor directing and criticising their work without charge.

The public interest resulted in his giving for the thousand dollars paid him for his Lowell Institute course of ten lectures, about five times the work expected; and it was evident to his friends that Dr. Rimmer was overworking. They advised his moving from Milton to some nearer suburb of Boston; but this he was unable to do for the want of money. The authorities of the Lowell Institute were asked to advance a portion of the sum already earned, but this request was refused upon the strict interpretation of a business contract. A lady, well known in Boston for her enthusiastic interest in education, was at this time an attendant upon Dr. Rimmer's lectures, and, becoming acquainted with these circumstances, loaned him five hundred dollars which an opportune legacy had put into her hands. It was only after much urging that he consented to receive the money, and then only with the distinct understanding that he should pay for its use. By the aid of this fund he removed from East Milton to Chelsea. His appreciation of the lady's kindness was evinced by his offer to receive, free of charge, any pupil she might send to his lectures or school.

That Dr. Rimmer's Institute lectures, if not richly paid, were yet not unappreciated, the following letter, written in March, 1864, may be taken as testimony : —

DR. WM. RIMMER.

*Dear Sir*, — We, the pupils of the Ladies' Class in Art Anatomy of the Lowell Institute, cannot close our lessons with you for the winter without expressing our deep sense of gratitude for the valuable instruction you have given us. Not restricting yourself to the hours engaged by the Lowell Institute, you have given up your time and strength to extra lessons in the class and at the Athenæum, which have increased many-fold the worth of the regular instruction. Your lessons in this city form a new era in the progress of art and education. By teaching drawing on the basis of scientific knowledge, you give it that certainty and power which no other method can; and all the greatest artists show us the necessity of that knowledge of anatomy which you are laboring to diffuse. By offering to women the same instruction and the same thorough training as to men, you have taken an important practical step in opening to them wider resources of intellectual and æsthetic culture, as well as remunerative industry. We cannot hope to repay you fully for what you have done for us; but we ask you to accept this collection of the great works of the poets of our mother tongue, as a proof of our respectful and grateful remembrance of your services.

We hope they will solace many a weary hour, and pleasantly remind you of the hours spent with your first public class in Boston.

Hoping that your health and strength may long be spared to continue your work, and that another winter may find us again assembled to profit by your instructions, we remain your attached and grateful pupils.

EDNAH CHENEY, *and Fifty Others.*


To this letter Dr. Rimmer returned the following reply : —

*To* MRS. EDNAH CHENEY, *and Others, members of the Ladies' Class in Art Anatomy of the Lowell Institute.*

LADIES, — I thank you sincerely for your excellent gift. The thing presented is before any other that which I should have hoped you might have selected for me, had I been apprised of your intentions; but, apart from its intrinsic worth, to be remembered by you in such kindly thoughts is to make your gift infinitely valuable.

I have indeed, as you say, given the same instruction to women as to men, because I believed and still believe that art intellectually is as independent of sex as thought itself.

And hence, believing that art ability is the same in women as men, I saw no reason why the same knowledge should not be conferred upon the one as well as the other.

The question of ability, if raised at all, can best be answered by referring to the books of both classes; while, if there is any argument in favor of the instruction of either sex, it must be for yours, which, from purely physical causes, is excluded from so many employments.

Thanking you for the patience with which you have followed me through the intricacies of so difficult a subject as art anatomy, and for the willingness with which you have listened to the severest strictures upon your work (that evidence of self-control which is so necessary an element in individual character, and in such a sphere as ours), hoping that it may be my pleasure to meet you all again under the patronage of an institution which has been the first, by the organization of the present classes, to admit the principles of high art among the elements of public instruction; and wishing you all many blessings,

I remain your humble servant,

WM. RIMMER.

Chelsea, March 28, 1864.

The success of Dr. Rimmer's lectures at the Lowell Institute had given rise to the hope that he might be permanently retained there, and a strong effort was made to secure the establishment of a school of art as a branch of the institution. This project failing, the male artists who had attended his lectures showed their grateful appreciation of his labors by the founding of a private art school, at the head of which he was placed. Col. E. C. Cabot, the architect, raised the sum of two thousand dollars with which to equip a schoolroom; and the following circular was issued: —

It is proposed to establish a school of drawing and modelling for artists and amateurs of both sexes, under the direction of Dr. William Rimmer.

There is now no place in New England where these studies can be pursued; and the talent which undoubtedly exists in the community either lies undeveloped, or exhibits a narrow and imperfect growth under imperfect discipline. Those persons who cannot avail themselves of foreign teaching are absolutely without the opportunities which experience has shown to be indispensable to a healthy school of art. To establish such a school, abundant facilities for study, both from life and from the antique, an organized system of classes and lectures, and eminent knowledge and skill on the part of the instructor, are essential requisites. The first of these can, of course, be provided at any time by a moderate expenditure of money, but the last has long been waited for in vain; and this enterprise would not now be undertaken, were it not for the favorable opportunity which Dr. Rimmer's singular qualifications afford. It is believed by persons most competent to judge, that a better professor of anatomy in its relations to art does not exist.

In the absence of such instruction, the study of drawing, in this community, has been of late years almost exclusively confined to landscape, and has, from the nature of the case, been mainly directed to those methods of handling by which the English and French schools have succeeded in imitating nature. Experience, however, has shown that for the cultivation of eye and hand, even in this branch of art, there is no discipline so efficient as that obtained from a study of the human figure. It is due not only to our artists themselves, but to the public, which shows a daily increasing disposition to recognize their merit, that what help can be got from training should be furnished them.

It is proposed to hire rooms, provide proper apparatus and accommodations for pupils, both as special students and in classes, under regulations that shall, as far as possible, meet the wants of all.

It is desirable, in order to facilitate the organization of the school, that persons wishing to join it should signify their intention to do so as soon as possible. This may be done, or further information obtained, by addressing a letter to Dr. Rimmer, at No. 54 Studio Building, Tremont Street, or by personal application to him there, between the hours of eleven and twelve any Monday, Wednesday, or Saturday.

| | |
|---|---|
| EDW. C. CABOT, | WM. M. HUNT, |
| J. HUNTINGTON WOLCOTT, | O. W. HOLMES, |
| MARTIN BRIMMER, | G. H. SHAW, |
| JEFFRIES WYMAN, | S. G. WARD, |
| GEO. B. EMERSON, | EDW. N. PERKINS. |
| J. E. CABOT, | |

BOSTON, Feb. 10, 1864.

The school opened with thirty-nine pupils, and continued with varying fortunes until the spring of 1866, when Dr. Rimmer removed to New York. It was his custom to give lectures on Saturday evening to those who were unable to pay the regular fees. He also taught many private pupils, his terms being a dollar an hour; and upon several occasions he lectured to Mrs. Ednah D. Cheney's ladies' class.

After coming to Chelsea he had joined the Freemasons, but he very rarely found time to attend the meetings of the order.

## CHAPTER IX.

### THE HAMILTON AND OTHER STATUES.

#### 1860-1865.

 NUMBER of persons who were fully convinced of Dr. Rimmer's ability as a sculptor were anxious that he should receive a commission for some public work. In 1864, largely through the exertions of Mr. Perkins, this desire was realized. Mr. Thomas Lee, a citizen of Boston, placed in the hands of Col. Cabot the sum of five thousand dollars, to be used in the erection of a granite statue of Alexander Hamilton; and to Dr. Rimmer was awarded the commission of executing the figure.

Col. Cabot had been from the first a warm and appreciative admirer of Dr. Rimmer. He believed, that, under congenial circumstances, the sculptor could produce grand works; and the existence of the St. Stephen and the Falling Gladiator certainly afforded sufficient ground for such a faith.

This was the first real art event of Dr. Rimmer's life. A successful statue of Hamilton would assure him all the commissions he wished, and open the way for grand ideal works. No fairer future was ever spread before a sculptor in this country than that which was now promised to Dr. Rimmer. Public interest, wealth, and sympathy were enlisted in his favor and anxious for his success; and reputation and independence seemed already secured. He engaged an unoccupied church in Chelsea, and made the clay model, between nine and ten feet in height, in eleven days in the month of December, 1864. As usual, he disdained or ignored all conveniences; the clay freezing and falling down so as to cause much additional labor, and no model being used. With some suggested perfecting of detail, the model was approved by the committee having the matter in charge, and was accordingly cut at Quincy in Concord granite. The completed statue was erected on

45

Commonwealth Avenue, in 1865, upon a pedestal of Quincy granite designed by Col. Cabot, which was ornamented by three medallion portraits in one panel — larger than life — of Washington, Hamilton, and Jay. The portraits were modelled by Dr. Rimmer, and for this he received twelve hundred dollars, — a generous price when compared with that paid for the figure.

Although the Hamilton family were much pleased with it, the statue of Hamilton was a disappointment to the public, and to the sculptor's friends as well. This disappointment was increased by some annoyances connected with its execution; and the result was to greatly lessen confidence in his ability as a sculptor of portraiture, and also to create a distrust of his capacity to execute work in which a large mass of material was an element. The feeling aroused was fatal to Dr. Rimmer's prospects as a sculptor, and he was not intrusted with any other public commission until 1875.

There were a few at that time, as at this, who were seriously impressed with the dignity, the repose, and the simple treatment of the HAMILTON. The late William M. Hunt found much in it to respect, and often spoke of its unappreciated merits. Artists who were forming opinions in regard to Dr. Rimmer's capacities had awaited its appearance as a crucial test. After its appearance, there were formed two widely differing estimates of his rank as an artist.

On the one hand it was asserted that Dr. Rimmer had developed as fully under the adverse influences of his place and time as would be possible under any circumstances; that his conceit, self-assertion, and sensitiveness prevented him from assimilating art nourishment; that the domestic side of his nature dominated over his allegiance to art; that he lacked that great essential, reserved power; that he had no loyalty to his art instinct, so that art, instead of being the sole aim and motive of his existence, the unconquerable necessity of his being, the medium for the deliverance of a divine message more important than life, was simply a convenient method of earning money, or a pleasant pastime for the passing moment. It followed, according to this view, that he could not respond to a great occasion, from the meagreness of his nature; that he could not continue the long struggle necessary for the consideration of a statue, but must do whatever he did at all quickly and without the long and concentrated effort from which alone has resulted whatever is great and noble in art.

Those who defended Dr. Rimmer took the ground that extreme hard work, suffering, and ill-health had exhausted his vitality to so great an extent that the long and continuous effort necessary for the production of a complete statue had become impossible to him; that the price, moreover, was not sufficient compensation for a more elaborate work; and that, so far as it attempts to go, the HAMILTON is of more value than any thing of which any other American was capable; that Dr. Rimmer had never received the encouragement he deserved, or which was given to inferior sculptors; and, finally, that no man could have done better under the circumstances.

I have not been able to learn whether the five thousand dollars was made to cover the expense of both statue and pedestal; but if this was the case, as thirty-two hundred were given to the granite company, only eighteen hundred would be left for the sculptor. Dr. Rimmer's family are under the impression that this was the fact, and that the price for the medallion was made larger upon this account. Speaking in his diary of the possibility of receiving the commission, the doctor writes: "Five thousand dollars is but half the amount that other sculptors receive for similar work; but it is best to do it for that price, for reputation."

Strangely enough, the sculptor was satisfied with his work, although he did observe, "If I were to make it again, I would finish the back with more care." He seemed equally unconcerned as to the injustice done to himself in hurrying the statue through in a few days, and to its probable effect upon future commissions. He had wasted the great opportunity of his life with an indifference which is marvellous.

My own opinion of the HAMILTON is, that it falls far short of being a full expression of the sculptor's ability, doing justice neither to himself nor to the public. It has, however, certain sterling qualities. Dr. Rimmer's aim was to produce an effect of dignity, of repose, of calm strength. The composition and style of execution is widely different from any other work which he executed, and of a kind in keeping with his aim. This fact, however imperfectly carried out, is indicative of a great art quality of mind, a sensibility to ideal impressions, and an effort to realize them in form. The statue has, moreover, that which no other statue in Boston possesses, — simplicity in conception and in execution, — merits of supreme value, and as rare as exalted. Had this been the work of a young sculptor, these merits and their suggestive possibilities would have warranted the belief in an unusual future eminence, yet probably would have been no more certain of wide acknowledgment at present than they have received in the HAMILTON.

To consider details, the head of the statue is well set upon the shoulders; the right arm, although hardly indicating itself as an arm, has a certain calm grace and direction that is admirable; the shoulders and upper part of body, while a little round, and lacking in nervous vigor, are suggestive of a fine, large sense of sculpture; while the back, with which so much fault has been found, although uninteresting, is neither ugly nor shocking; and the general scheme of the drapery is excellent.

As a whole, the HAMILTON is the indefinite work of a genius, who gave to its production moments where he should have given months. It is to be regretted that this should be the only public specimen of the sculptor's work. No other opportunity to engage in the production of public sculpture presented itself to the doctor, except through the occasional competition, — a process any thing but attractive to a serious artist as conducted in this country. On one occasion, from a sense of duty to his family, he called on a member of a public statue committee; but was refused an interview, being curtly informed that the statue was already contracted for. Such a reception was painful in the extreme to Dr. Rimmer, who felt that he had been insulted, and that in calling upon the person in question he had degraded himself. He made no more efforts to procure public work; though his proud nature endured many cruel moments when he saw other and inferior artists intrusted with important commissions, and himself passed disdainfully by.

Within the five years from February, 1860, to the close of 1865, Dr. Rimmer, in addition to his lectures and private instruction, made the model for the HAMILTON, and for four nude statues, three of them larger than life. These were the FALLING GLADIATOR, the CHALDEAN SHEPHERD, ENDYMION, and the OSIRIS.

The SHEPHERD and ENDYMION were modelled in East Milton, exhibited at the Boston Athenæum, and destroyed soon after. Photographs of them are too much faded for reproduction. The former was severely criticised at the time of its exhibition. The OSIRIS was made in Chelsea, immediately after the completion of the HAMILTON, in seven days; the sculptor, contrary to his custom, employing a living model, though for a few hours only, and simply for reference in completing the statue. It was designed to illustrate a different style of sculpture from that of the GLADIATOR, and one that the artist believed to be the highest, — a figure in repose. There were two heads to this figure, one a human, and the other that of a hawk, either one to be put on or taken off at pleasure. It was the doctor's favorite statue. The legs he especially admired. He preferred the hawk to the

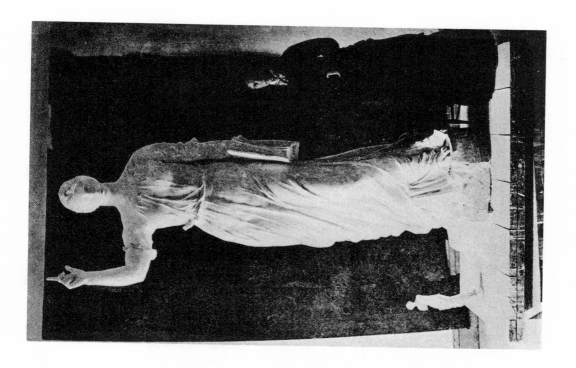

20. FAITH

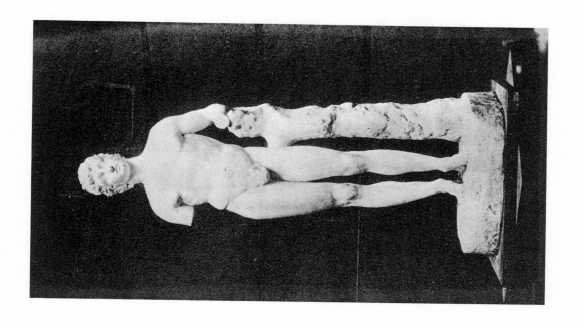

19. OSIRIS

21.  STATUE OF ALEXANDER HAMILTON

22.  SKETCH OF A YOUNG LIONESS

human head, thinking the latter too large. The photograph, of which a reproduction is given, did not please him.

The OSIRIS was exhibited at Childs and Jenks's gallery on Tremont Street with the hawk's head, but for a short time only, as objections were made to its nudity. The statue is admirable in many respects. The body is finely modelled, and there are some excellent qualities in the legs. The pose of the figure is elegant; it is chaste and suggestive, and shows a large feeling of sculpture. It looks like an antique. It is far superior to any nude work done before this time by any American, and of this style superior to any done since. If the gypsum figure of DESPAIR, the ST. STEPHEN, the GLADIATOR, the HAMILTON, and the OSIRIS were placed side by side, they would show, not only an extraordinary temperament for sculpture, but a variety which is wholly impersonal and the product of a very high order of imagination.

All of Dr. Rimmer's statues were executed, not as studies from nature, but as exemplifications of certain great principles of sculpture. The same principles have been repeatedly set forth by different sculptors in different periods, under the most favorable conditions; but here was a sculptor with every imaginable circumstance against him in his life and surroundings, living in a climate and community, and under a government, not only indifferent to art as such, but positively opposed to it as a human capacity in any broad sense or manner of expression; who felt those great art thoughts, and who succeeded in expressing them in a degree far beyond the point that had limited every other individual temperament in art as far as I know.

The OSIRIS was exhibited at the Cooper Institute, New York, while its author was at the head of the School of Design for Women in that institution, and for several years after, until broken and finally destroyed. Its destruction, however lamentable, must be set down to the side of the cruel inevitable that formed so large a part of the sculptor's career. Neither was there to be expected any lively general appreciation or interest in Dr. Rimmer as a producer of sculpture at the time in which he lived. He was out of his element in America, and might as well have produced his work in the wilds of Africa.

In answer to the question of a Boston artist, why he did not take more time in the execution of a nude figure, the doctor replied, " A week or two is all I need." The reply, with the fact that Rimmer invariably carried this principle into practice, is significant in all his art work except his painting. He executed with the utmost rapidity. He said his say at once, and, if not contented with his work, destroyed it.

During the first five years of his residence in Boston, he painted a number of pictures, and was employed to make several busts, although without notable success. One of these was a bust of Horace Mann, which he executed for Don Sarmiento, the president of the Argentine Confederacy, who desired to take with him to his country portraits of representative American educators. There was some misunderstanding in regard to this bust, which resulted in the annoyance of all concerned. A dark spot upon one cheek was objected to by Don Sarmiento, the doctor replying that "color was not an item in sculpture: old statues were discolored, yet that fact did not injure them."

## CHAPTER X.

### NEW YORK.

#### 1866-1870.

N 1866 Dr. Rimmer was invited by one of his pupils, a lady, to visit New York; and while there he was given a reception by Mrs. A. C. L. Botta, the distinguished poet and friend of art. Mrs. Botta also invited him to lecture at her house; and among the eminent citizens present at this lecture was Hon. Peter Cooper, the founder of the institute which bears his name.

The impression made by the doctor upon the minds of his hearers on this occasion was the same as he had produced five years before in Boston; and a movement was immediately inaugurated to induce him to come to New York as a lecturer. Mr. Cooper offered the use of a room in the institute, and Dr. Rimmer delivered a few lectures there.

These gave so much satisfaction that the trustees of the School of Design for Women, one of the art departments of the Cooper Institute, invited Dr. Rimmer to become its director and chief instructor. The school had not been conducted hitherto as satisfactorily as was desired; and it was thought by the trustees that if a capable artist was placed at its head, with full power of direction and supervision, the success of the school would be more certain. Dr. Rimmer accepted the invitation at a salary of three thousand dollars a year, with the understanding that he should procure whatever assistance he might need in the way of instructors, and pay them out of this sum. This engagement opened a wide field of labor, fair professional prospects, and a sure income. The method of instruction was left entirely to the doctor's regulation and supervision, and he had at length an opportunity to carry out freely his ideas concerning art education. As it had been in

Boston, so it was in New York. There had never been a teacher of art in that city so well equipped in a knowledge of the human figure. The principal and philanthropic object of the school was the education of young women in the various industrial arts, in order that they might become self-supporting. Dr. Rimmer at once began the task of arranging an elaborate course of study, with the view of establishing a permanent school. The plan of work is shown by the following circular : —

## COOPER UNION FOR THE ADVANCEMENT OF SCIENCE AND ART. SCHOOL OF DESIGN.

The School commences on the 1st of October, and closes on the 1st of June.

### COURSE OF INSTRUCTION.

Drawing from casts.
Drawing from life.
Painting in oil and water-colors.
Design and composition.
Modelling in clay.
Elementary principles for teachers.
Lectures upon art anatomy.
Composition, anatomy, etc.
Lectures upon systematic and structural botany.
Lectures upon primitive forms; viz., action, motion, proportion, etc.
Lectures upon manners, customs, implements.

### RULES.

The school-hours are from nine A.M. to one P.M., Saturdays excepted.
The lecture-hours are from twelve to one daily.
The course of instruction is progressive.
The students are advanced from step to step by the director.
Students cannot select the departments of study.
Students are expected to attend school for one class year, no person being admitted for a shorter time.
Persons wanting in diligence, or whose deportment is exceptional, or who are found to be deficient in talent, are not retained in the School.
Pupils furnish their own drawing and painting materials.

Casts, easels, and clay are furnished by the School.

There is a public exhibition of the works of the students at the close of each class year.

No work can be removed from the school premises until after the exhibition, except for special reasons satisfactory to the trustees or director.

Satisfactory reference as to character must be given before being admitted as a student.

Visitors are admitted on Fridays, no person being allowed to visit the School at other times except by special permission from a trustee, lady of the Advisory Council, or curator.

Pupils are not required to pay any entrance-fee, and the instruction is gratuitous.

ABRAM S. HEWITT, *Secretary.*
W. RIMMER, M.D., *Director.*

This comprehensive and varied programme Dr. Rimmer undertook to carry out in a school numbering from one hundred to two hundred pupils, without any professional assistance except that given by the more advanced students and those who were preparing to become teachers. It was an immense, an unparalleled undertaking. There might be other men who would assume the accomplishment of a similar enterprise, but it is doubtful if any man who ever lived could carry it through satisfactorily. So far as enthusiasm, ambition, enormous power of work, courage, and knowledge could go, Dr. Rimmer was sure of more than ordinary success. He had worked enormously in Boston, but this New-York course would have given ample employment to an entire corps of instructors. The majority of the pupils were under twenty years of age; some of them had followed their instructor from Boston: and there were constantly more applicants than could be accommodated. The scheme of discipline was thoroughly systematic, the older pupils acting as monitors. Draped models were employed when necessary. Ideal busts and figures in sculpture were made without models. Private day and evening classes were formed, Dr. Rimmer conducting them without additional remuneration. His lectures upon art anatomy were much the same as those delivered in Boston. He fully understood that practical and definite results were expected from the school, and his aim was to teach his pupils to help themselves. A teachers' society was formed, with Dr. Rimmer as president, for the double purpose of better preparing those pupils who desired to become teachers, and of securing employment for those who were ready to assume this responsibility, or sufficiently advanced to begin practical work. The art of wood-engraving was added to the list of studies, this department being under the direction of Mr. W. J. Linton, a distinguished English engraver; and the following circular was issued, calling the attention of the New-York publishers to this fact : —

## COOPER UNION FOR THE ADVANCEMENT OF SCIENCE AND ART.

The undersigned would respectfully inform the publishers of New York that the ladies of the engraving department of the School of Design in the Cooper Union are prepared to receive orders for wood-engraving at very reasonable rates. Some of the members of this department have long been known as engravers of superior ability, and all are persons of fair average talent and experience; and the undersigned does not hesitate to say, considering the excellence of the work produced, and the price charged for it, that publishers will be greatly benefited by any patronage bestowed upon the school. Specimens may be seen at the engraving-room any day except Saturday.

Hours from ten to twelve A.M., and from three to four P.M.

Respectfully,

W. RIMMER,
*Director School of Design.*

The School of Design soon gained a worthy public distinction. Distinguished educators from different parts of this country and Europe visited it, and were warm in their praise of the great work it was accomplishing in art education. Its pupils went to all parts of the country as teachers. Others became distinguished as artists. Every thing which the fertile brain of its director could imagine for the benefit of his classes was done. To all intents and purposes the school was his own, the pupils being to him as his own children, their success occupying all his thought.

Dr. Rimmer was, as he might well be, jealous of his department at the Cooper Institute, and ready at all times to defend it. The following letters were written in reply to some criticisms of " The New-York Tribune : " —

*To the Editor of " The Sun."*

SIR, — In yesterday's " Tribune," some one has spoken very frankly of the School of Design in the Cooper Union; and as nothing is better for any student, let the sphere of labor be what it may, than earnest and sincere criticism, the writer has in this contributed his share toward the advancement of art, and for this he has the thanks of all concerned. It is of little consequence that many in whom we all have greater confidence, and who, in our opinion, are better qualified to judge, differ from the writer as to the year's work, and the value of the methods adopted in the school. What is of more consequence to us is, that we should have the benefit of good advice, whenever and wherever it may be had; and I therefore most

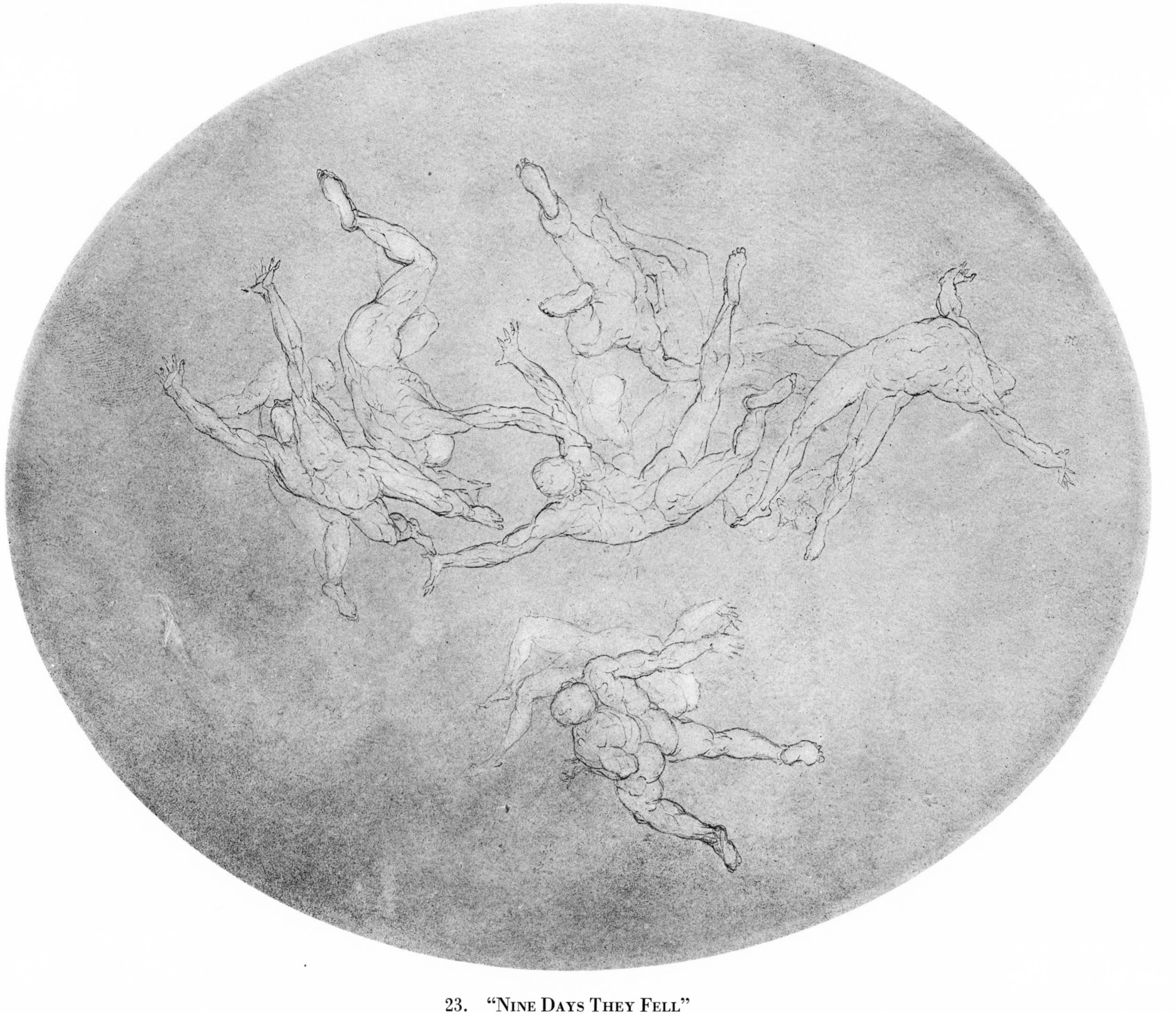

23. "Nine Days They Fell"

respectfully offer the writer the use of the lecture-room of the School of Design for as many hours, day or evening, as he may think necessary, that he may give us the benefit of any knowledge he may possess, or any opinion he may have formed, concerning the best course to pursue in the adoption of elementary principles and methods in a school of design. Any opinions he may choose to advance shall have the fullest attention and the most careful examination, and shall be acted upon without equivocation as soon as the school opens in the fall, if found to possess any particular merit. If the writer does not choose to give us the benefit of his knowledge and opinions in a lecture or course of lectures, I should be glad to hear from him in private, and will furnish him every facility for studying the system of instruction now in practice; and the school, if he desires it, shall be open to him at all times without reserve. As he may not have been informed as to the course now adopted in the female department, I cut from the school circular the following items. [See circular on p. 52.]

The writer says, "It may seem unkind to speak so bluntly about the work of a hundred or more girls, if it did not seem unkind to keep silent." The *way* in which a thing may be said is altogether a matter of taste; and in view of what has been said, and the *way* in which it has been said, it has been thought that the pupils of the school can bear that such things should be said as well as the writer can bear to say them. The writer says again: "The school of design has been merely a third-rate drawing-school." As art is especially an outgrowth of taste and sentiment, we can give no offence by saying that tastes differ, and that we will find a person connected with the school who will decline no trial of artistic strength in any department of knowledge or taste that he may offer.

Hoping to hear from him at an early day in regard to the time when he may choose to favor us with his opinions in detail,

I remain yours with respect,

W. RIMMER,
*Director of the School of Design for Women.*

NEW YORK, June 2, 1868.

*To the Editor of the Tribune.*

SIR, — On the 1st of June there appeared an article in "The Tribune" which made a severe attack upon the teaching and management of the School of Design for Women at the Cooper Institute. The article referred to was very severe upon the work of the pupils recently exhibited.

There is one point where your writer has damaged the institution, and I should regret to think "The Tribune's" influence would intentionally be thrown against an educational movement of the right sort. There is in the school a teachers' class, composed of the more advanced pupils: its object is to train young women to support themselves as teachers of art. The writer of your article lays special stress on the improbability of any young woman from the Cooper School ever being able "to earn her own living," and regrets that the original plan of training, designing for manufacturing patterns, should have been abandoned.

It is advertised in "The Tribune" that competent teachers can be had in various departments from this advanced class. It is also virtually advertised, through the article alluded to, that such teachers are utterly incompetent, and that young ladies who expect any good in art had better avoid the Cooper teaching and system. Whether any good is likely to come from this school, or any young woman be trained "to earn her own living" through her studies there, I would merely remark that my daughter, a pupil of two years' standing, has received repeated offers, one thousand to twelve hundred dollars per annum, as a teacher of drawing. There is no need of her accepting these proposals; but, having sent her there to be trained for such work, as a great many other young women have been, it is some satisfaction to be able to say the time spent at this school has not been wholly lost in her case. Mr. Cooper did a good thing in founding this institution. Dr. Rimmer is doing a good thing in aiming to establish a school of art that shall be a credit to the city.

I am, sir,

Very truly yours,　　　　　　　　B.

New York, June 10, 1868.

At the annual exhibition the results of the year's work were examined by the trustees of the school, and by a large number of visitors. They comprised, upon the average, over four hundred specimens of drawing, painting, and wood-engraving, and nearly thirty pieces of sculpture. In addition to the regular prizes given annually, Dr. Rimmer himself provided two gold medals, — one for excellence in modelling, and the other for greatest progress in all branches. The latter bore this inscription, " *Qui non proficit, deficit* " ("He who does not advance, goes backward").

Dr. Rimmer remained in charge of this school until the close of the term ending June 1, 1870. After the first year, he received a salary of four thousand dollars. For the first two years matters went on well, and, as before remarked, the school assumed an importance perceptibly felt in the community; but during the last year or two it became evident to the trustees that still greater progress was necessary, and that the school must be re-organized. There were two elements in Dr. Rimmer's system which must inevitably prove irreconcilable. These were the single personal government, as represented by its director, and the impossibility of his properly attending to the necessities of each pupil. The first element was thought by the trustees to be too unyielding in its administration, and the latter not ample enough to meet the requirements of the school. It is affirmed that he did not follow with sufficient care the original intention of the school, which was to instruct in industrial, rather than fine art. The young women were required to execute large and elaborate compositions in painting and sculpture, more from knowledge than from an intimate and constant reference to nature. This method of work aroused much adverse criticism: the value of its immediate or eventual results was questioned. Dr. Rimmer always insisted that "all the students of the school should be brought under the influence of one mind." Experience has long since demonstrated that no one mind, however strong, can long conduct successfully an art school of such magnitude. The trustees made some suggestions to the doctor regarding this aspect of the subject; but he found it difficult to understand them, or to change his course. "The trustees were not artists," was his ground: "how could they look at this matter from so high a standpoint as he did?"

Public criticism in some instances took sides with the trustees. This annoyed and pained Dr. Rimmer; calling in question as it did his capacity as an artist and teacher, and, as he thought, endangering the prosperity of the school.

The difference of opinion between Dr. Rimmer and the trustees increased rather than diminished; and in the winter of 1869–70, there seeming no way of reconciling these antagonisms, a change in the conduct of the school was decided upon. The following characteristic anecdote illustrates the state of affairs at this time. Mr. Hewitt, visiting the classes one day, said to the director, —

"You are a remarkable man, Dr. Rimmer, but a hard man to manage."

"I came here," replied the other, "to manage this school, not to be managed myself."

Before the beginning of the next school year, a lady was appointed to take charge of the business portion of Dr. Rimmer's former duties, he being invited to the position of lecturer on anatomy and the principles of art; his work to occupy two hours of each day, and his salary to be two thousand dollars a year. For this sum the doctor could not think of remaining in New York, and the offer was finally increased to three thousand dollars for three hours of daily work.

It does not appear that there was in the minds of the trustees any doubt of the value of Dr. Rimmer's services during the four years he remained at the Cooper Institute, — of his self-sacrificing enthusiasm, or his readiness to do all in his power for the success of the school; and, indeed, their offer of the position of lecturer is sufficient proof of their confidence in his ability and sincerity.

To occupy a subordinate position in a public institution, where he had been its chief for years; to know and daily feel that his former authority was divided with others, chosen independently of his selection and without his sanction, and whom he could not regard but as his inferiors, — was a requirement that his proud spirit could not endure for an instant. He thought, if there were any changes to be made in the scheme of studies and in the selection of teachers, it was his right as director of the school to be consulted. He was willing and desirous to select assistants who would co-operate with him, but any change in his plan he regarded as fatal. He had understood from Mr. Cooper that "all would go on in the future as in the past;" but on returning to New York in the autumn, to resume, as he thought, his old position, he found the re-organization of the school to be an accomplished fact. His surprise and disappointment were overwhelming. His hope of founding a school of fine art went out in despair. Relentless fate again appeared to him, and for the first time in his life he felt that old age was creeping upon him. Wearied with the uncertainties of human experience, exhausted in body, and sick in soul, he closed his heart to professional allurements for the last time. Henceforth bread should be his only solicitude. He tried to overlook what he considered a humiliation, and to consider favorably the offer of three thousand dollars. He also made an effort to secure pupils for a private class, that his income might be sufficient for the needs of his family. This last was, however, not practicable, and the first was impossible. His sensitive nature and his artistic pride had received too severe a shock. He desired to be "sole director of a school of art, not a teacher in one department." He declined the offer, and returned to Boston, where he began preparations for opening a private school.

It is difficult, perhaps impossible, to estimate correctly the beneficial results of the sculptor's teaching at the Cooper Institute. Many think that the time he left his directorship was the most critical moment in the career of the school. Not only had it vastly improved under his supervision, but the system laid out by him required a much longer time for full trial, to prove its own superiority, and test his capacity. His faithful friend Mr. Perkins advised Dr. Rimmer to remain in New York, considering that city more generous and public-spirited than Boston; but the latter city was the doctor's old home, he had many friends and admirers there, his house was in Chelsea, and he chose to trust his future to the place which had been the scene of his early struggles.

24. VICTORY

The intention of Dr. Rimmer in the Institute school is deserving of all praise. He undertook what would have been too much in any branch of education, and which in that of fine art seems almost foolhardy. Yet his mistake must be attributed to the high value he placed upon art education, the lofty standard of his own nature, and his noble desire to be useful to mankind, and not to any petty love of notoriety or vain-glory. The same imperious will that would brook no suggestion, or suffer deviation in its course, was an essential inspiration in the execution of the interesting work that he has left behind him. It was as positive and undeviating with men as with granite.

While at the Cooper Institute, the doctor had found time to remodel the CHALDEAN SHEPHERD and the ENDYMION; but neither was cast in plaster, and both were soon destroyed. He also painted a number of pictures, — one of them, CUPID RELATING HIS ADVENTURES TO VENUS, was exhibited in Boston and New York. Its color was severely criticised, and the artist afterward painted an English landscape over it.

On several occasions the director was the recipient of valuable testimonials from his students. For private pupils his terms were fifty dollars a month, two lessons being given weekly. One wealthy student, to show his appreciation of his instructor's worth and kindness, tripled this sum; and the members of his classes not infrequently presented him with gifts. One of these, " The Iconographic Encyclopædia," was accompanied by this note: —

*To our dear Teacher*, DR. RIMMER.

We are very happy to offer you, on your birthday, something we think you will value. It is the gift of the whole school, the free-will offering of hearts that are mindful of the patience and kindness of your daily teachings; and we think it would please you to know how the idea suggested itself here and there in quiet corners, and how eagerly all have sought to share the pleasure of giving. By this token, your pupils send you an affectionate greeting to-day, and wish you many golden years to come.

Respectfully,

CLASS OF 1867 AND '68.

In New York Dr. Rimmer made the acquaintance of many eminent people, enjoyed many social pleasures, and the four years spent there he called the happiest of his life.

# CHAPTER XI.

## BOSTON.

### 1870–1876.

THE project of founding a school which should embody and carry into operation his principles and methods of art instruction had been the strongest desire of Dr. Rimmer's life ; and although with the failure of his plans at the Cooper Institute he seemed to abandon all hope of a full realization of this, he still made one more attempt in Boston. Soon after his return from New York he made the necessary arrangements, and sent out the following circular : —

## ART ANATOMY.

Dr. Rimmer, having withdrawn from the directorship of his School of Design in New York (an office held by him for the last four years), desires respectfully to inform his friends and the public, that he will resume his classes in Boston, at Hall No. 21 (for the present) Wesleyan Association Building, Bromfield Street. Class days, Mondays, Wednesdays, and Fridays, from ten to twelve, A.M.

Dr. Rimmer solicits attention to the fact, that this is the only school in the country in which art anatomy in connection with sculpture and painting, and ethnology in its relations to art, are taught. In returning to Boston, he does so with the intention of making such a school as shall supply to the art student all that mere instruction can give.

Particular attention will be paid to the education of the young, and the elementary principles suitable for them will be thoroughly and faithfully taught; it being his first object in all branches, and through all the details of instruction, to develop the artistic faculty, and to quicken and educate the sensibilities in every thing relating to it.

25.   SKETCH OF A HORSE

26.   HORSES OF THE CHARIOT OF THE SUN

27.   FENCING LESSON

28.   DEAD SOLDIER

The course of instruction is as follows : —

*Comparative Anatomy.* — Forms of animals; peculiarities of animals; men and animals combined.

*Human Anatomy.* — Skeleton outlines and parts, with names. Infant outline and development; female outline and development; male outline and development; names, forms, attachment, and uses of muscles; expression, latent and passionate; comparison of the heads of the different races of men and of animals; proportion, foreshortening, elementary perspective, elementary principles for teachers; object-drawing, moulding in clay, landscape sketching; lectures on architecture, manners, customs, implements.

This being the course of instruction adopted by Dr. Rimmer in the School of Design, New York, of the pupils of which institution he was the sole art instructor.

Terms, ten dollars per month, payable in advance.

P.S. — Students advised in regard to works executed out of school, without additional charge.

Pupils taken in classes from private schools at reduced rates.

In his newspaper advertisement of the school, Dr. Rimmer inserted the following extract from an article published in " The Boston Sunday Herald : " —

" M. Armand Dumaresq was a commissioner sent two years ago by the French government to examine the educational institutions of the country. His remarks upon the methods of Dr. William Rimmer, then superintendent of the School of Design in the Cooper Institute, are highly complimentary. We translate in substance from his report, which has just been printed.

" He says, ' In order to give me an idea of his mode of instruction, Dr. Rimmer drew a chimpanzee head with surprising facility, presented the African and Caucasian types, then the different modifications from childhood to manhood, the difference between the head of man and of woman, coming at last to the female head, which changes with age towards a masculine character. All these drawings are executed during the explanations. The demonstration, with proof in hand, is charming and profitable for the pupil, especially in a country where the study of nature is not allowed to women beyond the head and extremities. A theoretical method was required, and great difficulties had to be overcome. Perceiving the results obtained with his pupils, who are advanced far enough to model large, naked, well-composed statues, the anatomy of which is perfect, it was beyond contradiction that a difficult problem had been solved here. His method is based on the profound study of the antique and the Italian masters, as well as of nature. Dr. Rimmer is a teacher who is really a master of his art. I complimented him very highly, and I do not hesitate to say that I should be happy to see a similar teacher in France.'"

Dr. Rimmer's school opened with twenty pupils; and from this time until its close, the autumn of 1876, the average attendance was about the same. Perhaps the most interesting experience of the artist in this connection was with his children's class. He was very fond of children. "We live our lives over again in our children," he wrote to his daughter, "and must enter into all their joys and sorrows as our own;" and his desire to start them correctly and intelligently in drawing and the practice of art shows one of his most delightful characteristics, as well as his broad capacity as an art teacher. His method with them was that already described as employed in his adult classes. "The unison, quickness, and intelligence displayed in these exercises," he writes, "were as remarkable as they were correct; and the children became fairly wild with enthusiasm." Even in this class the doctor insisted upon the attempt to express an idea, in preference to exactitude in copying.

During Dr. Rimmer's absence from Boston, his fame as a lecturer had considerably increased; and upon his return to that city, in 1870, to open his private school, he received invitations to lecture before a number of educational institutions and art societies.

In January, 1866, he had been invited by members of the National Academy of Design to lecture in their building to the artists of the city. He appeared upon the platform at the hour appointed; but the chalk and blackboards proved unfit for use, and the light insufficient. The lecture was, however, begun, and a few drawings made that were received with applause by a fair-sized audience; but the lecturer felt that he could not do justice to himself under the circumstances, and closed the lecture with his regrets. In the winter of 1871–72 he was asked to give twenty-five lectures to the members and students of the same institution for the sum of one thousand dollars. Two lectures were to be given each week; but, after delivering sixteen, the doctor wished to give them more frequently, in order to close the course at an earlier date than at first intended. The authorities opposed this change, as the artists desired sufficient time between the lectures to properly study those previously given. No arrangement mutually satisfactory could be arrived at; and the lectures ended there, much to the regret of the artists, who expressed their appreciation of "the unique character of the lectures and of their inestimable value."

The Technological School of Worcester, Mass., also invited Dr. Rimmer to

29.   SECESSIA AND COLUMBIA

30.   TO THE 54TH REGIMENT MASSACHUSETTS VOLUNTEERS

deliver twelve lectures before the faculty and students.    Report says, " These lectures were thinly attended, owing to the fact that the doctor was not sufficiently known."

In 1872 the lecturer delivered an address before the Yale School of Fine Arts: he was also asked to lecture in Burlington, at the University of Vermont, but did not, because of its distance from Boston.  On the invitation of Mrs. John M. Forbes of Milton, he lectured once a week at her house to a party of her friends for three months, beginning Nov. 6, 1875, and again in the winter of 1876–77, for a like period. Mrs. Forbes provided two blackboards ; and, at her request, the doctor did not rub out the last drawings of each lecture.  She traced them on thin paper, and then transferred them to cloth for preservation ; thus making a collection of a hundred or more interesting examples, large and small, of his drawings.  They are the only specimens of the kind that are positively known to be in existence.  I have been told by several persons, that the drawings made while the doctor occupied rooms in the Studio Building in Boston were photographed with the intention of preserving them ; but, in spite of repeated endeavors, I have been unable to find them.  As in very many instances of thoughtful appreciation, and loyal, beautiful tribute paid during his life and after his death, Dr. Rimmer receives a peculiarly agreeable one, through the considerate interest of a woman, in the preservation of the Milton drawings.

In the winter of 1875–76, beginning Dec. 10 and closing Feb. 25, Dr. Rimmer was engaged to deliver ten lectures at the Normal Art School in Boston.  The conditions under which these lectures were given were any thing but agreeable.  He abhorred the system taught in the school ; and the conveniences provided for the delivery of the lectures were so unsatisfactory that he wrote a letter of complaint to its director.  In first draught, this letter read as follows ; but it was probably modified before being sent : —

MR. WALTER SMITH.

*Dear Sir*, — It will be impossible for me to complete the course with the blackboard now used, to say nothing of the somewhat " ticklish " arrangement for a platform.  As matters now stand, my reputation and my neck are alike in danger ; for I can neither stand securely nor draw correctly.  Pushing the box about from one end of the board to another is the proper business of a scene-shifter.  If I am to do it, I must ask for extra pay : to be shifter and draughtsman is rather too much, even for me.  I must observe that the light is reflected from the surface of the blackboard in such a way as to make it necessary that I should stand sideways before I can see my own work.  The crack in the board, you may observe, comes in the wrong place.  I must ask for better arrangements.

On occasions when Dr. Rimmer's temper was disturbed, he did not so often express himself by word of mouth as by inditing an epistle to the cause of his annoyance. Sometimes these letters were sent; at others, thrown aside, with the remark, "No: it's better to say nothing, and let things take their course." The following amusing correspondence passed between himself and Mr. Walter Smith. The latter had been employed by the Commonwealth of Massachusetts to establish and direct a system of art education, including a State Normal Art School for the training of teachers of drawing and design.

### MR. SMITH TO DR. RIMMER.

BOSTON, Nov. 22, 1876.

DEAR SIR, — Will you please inform me what is the distinction you make between *structural* and *art* anatomy.

Yours very truly,

WALTER SMITH.

### EXTRACTS FROM DR. RIMMER'S REPLY.

DEAR SIR, — In the introduction to Cruveilhier's " Anatomy," editor's preface, is the following, which may perhaps be quite as satisfactory as any thing that might be offered from any other source : —

"Structural anatomy is anatomy viewed abstractly and without reference to its connections with physiology, pathology, or the practice of medicine or surgery."

A very dry study, as the editor intimates. The word "structural" means anatomy in the abstract, as the word "function" means function in the abstract, even though their correlation may be inseparable as you know. If anatomy may be viewed abstractly and without reference to physiology, . . . it may be without reference to art.

Art anatomy relates, not only to structural anatomy, but to the form of the whole body, as representative of a type of man or animal; to the changes of form resulting from, and incidental to, the uses of the several parts of the body, upon the basis of the structural relation.

To the form of the body during infancy; to the female body; to the male body; to animal or structural expression; to proportion in general, and as embodied in different individuals, as embodied in works of art; to the change wrought in the whole body by changes wrought in parts of the body; to types of mankind; . . . to the several details in each department of a subject, illustrated by good and sufficient drawings. . . .

In Dr. Rimmer's note-book, this item is found under date 1871: "A class of twenty want me at Harvard College."

There is no record, however, of his having given instruction of any kind at the college after the lectures of 1865, before mentioned.

In the autumn and winter of 1874, and again in 1875, he took charge of a night drawing-school in the city of Chelsea, where he resided, receiving for this service $315.50 and $335. He was also a member of the school committee for the former year, but declined further service, although re-elected.

About this time he gave a short course of lectures to a number of artists, who met in Mr. L. G. Schirmer's room in the Studio Building. At another time an invitation was extended him from the photographers of Boston to favor them with a lecture upon the character, power, and importance of light. "It was accepted," one of them remarks; "and a most delightful and profitable evening was passed in listening to his profound observations upon this important subject." He also visited occasionally Miss H. M. Knowlton's Young Women's Art School, to lecture or give other art instruction.

# CHAPTER XII.

## PROVIDENCE.

### 1871-1873.

R. RIMMER also gave a course of twelve lectures in Providence, R.I., beginning Oct. 24, 1871, stopping, as he passed through that city, on his way from New York to Boston. Some of the details of this and of two subsequent courses, delivered by him in Providence, are deserving of permanent record.

The delivery of the first course was due chiefly to the interest and exertions of a few ladies, Miss Katherine H. Austin being one of the most active. The lectures were given before a class of about twenty ladies and gentlemen. The second course began Jan. 28, and closed April 8, 1872.

In the autumn of the same year, Col. Charles A. Nichols, a public-spirited citizen of Providence, entered heartily into the project of securing Dr. Rimmer's services for a third course of lectures. He solicited subscriptions from others, and generously subscribed himself for those who were not able to pay. The use of a room in the High-school Building — now the Normal School — was given for these lectures, which began Dec. 28, 1872. They were attended by the representative citizens of the city, as well as by artists and amateurs. Dr. Rimmer's price per course was six hundred dollars; but he was willing to accept the amount raised — about four hundred dollars — for each course. The Providence lectures, thirty-six in number, are the only ones that were ever reported for the press; being written out by Miss Austin, Col. Nichols, and Miss Rosa F. Peckham, the artist, for " The Providence Journal."

I have selected twelve of these reports, which of course are abstracts, and not full records of the speaker's words : —

## 1.

The introductory lecture of this course was delivered last Monday afternoon at the Normal School. The lecturer commenced with a review of the different standards of form in animal and man, and of the progress of structural development from animal to man, the growth from infancy to manhood, and from the young to the mature animal; citing examples, and illustrating his statements by drawings. From these we learn that the spinal column, curved in the adult man, is nearly straight in infancy. Wherever in the child there is to be a future growth of muscle, we find large masses of integument. In women the development of the muscular system is arrested, rarely exceeding that of a boy of twelve years. All young animals have skulls large in proportion to their bodies. The height of man is eight times the length of the head, that of an infant only four.

This was followed by some remarks on proportion. In the adult, the length from the knee to the ground is equal to the length of the body which occupies half the distance from the knee to the sternum. This proportion obtains only in the best Greek statues, and in the most finely shaped men, ordinarily the body being longer in proportion. An analysis comparing the distinguishing human and animal peculiarities was given, showing upon what expression depends. The skull of an ape, which the lowest human types resemble, has all the characteristics of the human skull. The classic head represents the opposite extreme. As a countenance approaches either one of these types, we call it animal or intellectual. An animal skull is distinguished by exceedingly great depth from the crown to the upper maxillary section, which gives room for attachment of immense muscles of the neck, an organization peculiar to pugilists, — hence the resemblance of fighting animals, as the bull-dog, — and incompatible with a large, sensitive brain.

R. F. P.

## II.

Continuing a review of the subject of expression, the lecturer, by drawings of brute and human skulls, illustrated the animal and human distinctions, and pointed out the characteristic differences of each feature. In the animal the frontal section is depressed and hollowed, and not on the same plane with the nasal section, which is flat; super-orbital section prominent, malar bones marked; nostrils flat, opening forward; large projecting muscle about the mouth, chin retreating, and the line of the jaw depressed and hollowed upward. Woman is an example of the arrest of development, — retaining childlike and infantile peculiarities. The broad shoulders, beard, powerful limbs, the large hand, indicate an increased development of the animal in man. In art, woman represents emotion and sentiment: and, in comparing types, she is the highest representative, not only of emotion and sentiment, but of intellect also; the brain of woman is, proportionably, the largest of any created being. The average weight of woman is one-quarter to one-third less than that of man, while the average weight of the brain is only four ounces less.

Taking, then, the skull of the woman as the highest type, the opposite extreme of the animal, we find the frontal eminence convex, the nasal section projecting, the cutaneous section about the mouth small, the mucous section, which is entirely wanting in the animal, large, the chin projecting, and the cranium large, round, and full; the distance from the top of the skull to a line drawn through the eye, equalling the distance from the eye to the chin. Strength is the highest characteristic of the animal, of which the gorilla is the best representative. Drawings of the comparative anatomy of the lion and gorilla showed that the latter far excelled the former in size and strength. Animals possess none of those properties which are able to bring us into communication with them. A man who is ignorant of music, sculpture, or painting, is a stranger, in respect to those arts, to the musician, sculptor, or artist, and is incapable of communicating with either. As a man's power of communication increases, he becomes less of an animal.

The lecture closed with a series of drawings representing a head of the lowest type, developed through various ascending stages to a purely human head, the last still retaining all the characteristics of the original type.

R. F. P.

## III.

In the third lecture of this course, the lecturer proceeded in the elucidation of the various mysterious phases of the human countenance which determine the character and expression of the individual. The different planes of the nasal bones indicate the degree which the head occupies in the scale of development; the lowest type having the plane nearly horizontal, and the highest nearly vertical. In accordance with the custom of the antique sculptors, who, in the representation of their gods, magnified all purely human characteristics, we find the head of *Jupiter Tonans* exaggerated in this respect. The plane of a head of the highest type is vertical, and may be indicated by 100°. The plane of the head of Jupiter, according to the same standard, would be indicated by 110°.

The European head has high nasal bones, small zygomatic arch and malar bones, and approaches the nearest to the highest type, from which each nation has its own peculiar form of deviation. The characteristic American head has high cheek-bones, and a large muscle about the wide, flat mouth. This was illustrated by a drawing of the head in question, which, with its air of keenness, alertness, and acumen, might well stand as a representation of the conventional Western politician, although bearing a strong individual resemblance to Henry Clay. In Vermont the heads do not vary in the usual manner: one often sees among the farmers heads approaching the English type. California is said to develop heads of a high order, as well as fine physiques, although the average height is less. In New England the

31. AND SATAN CAME ALSO

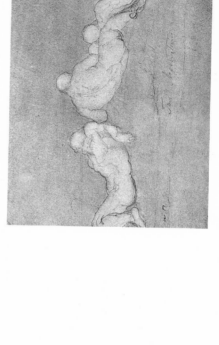

32. MORNING—FEMALE FIGURE

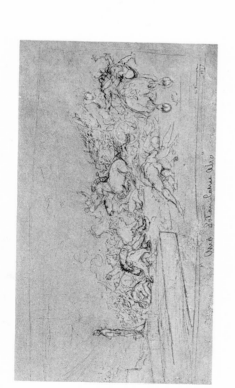

33. DEDICATED TO THE
44TH REGIMENT MASSACHUSETTS VOLUNTEERS

34. TRI-MOUNTAIN

English debased head is of a very brutal character, and persons with such heads are found to be not at all amenable to the influences of civilization. The head of any nation in its deterioration approaches the aboriginal type, as shown by the English in New Zealand, and the American debased head, approximating to the Indian type. Illustrations were given explaining these resemblances, and showing the debased head of other nations, — of the French head, which bore a strong likeness to the gorilla; of the Irish head, which, in its highest development, affords some of the finest examples of the purely human type; and of the Aztec head as found on ancient monuments, which appeared to be *sui generis*, differing in its depravity from any other given type. Caricatures always represent mobs with debased heads, embodying most of these points. Familiarity with the various types enables us to discriminate the peculiarities of the individual head, and teaches us wherein it falls short of perfection.

The highest and lowest heads have a characteristic outline of the profile, and an equally characteristic *inner* outline formed by the zygomatic arch, the malar bone, nostril, and the integument about the mouth, which in the animal face is pushed far back by the large muscle, orbicular oris, the mouth itself being wide and flat. We often see a junction of the high and low type outline of the profile. A high-type profile, the silhouette of which would convey the idea of a perfect head, is sometimes degraded by having its inner outline of the animal type. Heads of low type have often an inner outline of the higher type, as in the case of some negroes and the Mound Indian.

The occipital bone marks the character of the head. If short, the spinal marrow enters the brain obliquely, throwing the head forward, as in apes. If long, it enters vertically, and the head cannot be otherwise than vertical.

A head of the highest type, resembling Julius Cæsar, was sketched, the under lip protruding after the manner of fighting animals, the forehead on a more inclined plane than the nasal sections, the whole exhibiting marked leonine features, and demonstrating the fact that the finest heads may have certain animal characteristics. Structural peculiarities were shown to be quite as prominent seen from behind. In the savage, the cerebral section is larger at the base, and angular at the top, instead of rounded as in the civilized man; the neck short, the masseter muscle projecting largely, the shoulders concave, and not convex as in the higher races. The neck of woman is longer, her shoulders never so large as man's; but the short neck, lower occiput, and many other animal traits in man, render woman the highest type.

The artistic difference to be observed between the highest and lowest type of heads is the preponderance of the facial over the cerebral section in the purely animal head, and of the cerebral over the facial section in the purely human head.

R. F. P.

## IV.

The lecturer took up the subject of the pectoral muscles, showing their relation to the deltoid muscle, and the manner of their attachment to the pectoral eminence of the humerus, explaining also that these muscles are composed of fibres which fold upon each other in such a manner that they are only exhausted in case of extreme tension of the arm. These fibres end in the aponeurotic tendon which attaches the muscles to the bone. The pectoral was shown to be one of the most important sections of the body in its relation to other parts. In designing a figure, the body may be made short, but the shoulders should be broad, exceeding in width the length of the body, which occupies one-third the distance from the top of the sternum to the ground. These proportions are sanctioned by the best Greek masters. The lecturer found them to obtain, by actual measurement, in fifteen of the finest statues of antiquity; the *Athlete* of the Vatican being the only exception. Dramatic statues are never so difficult to achieve as those in perfect repose. Motion disturbs the sense of proportion, and it is not easy to say of a limb in action whether the proportion is right or wrong. Perfect repose is far more difficult to express. To make a figure truly fine, the motion must be latent. If the arms are brought together, the breadth of the shoulders is disturbed. Not only the position, but the defining of the muscles, disturbs harmony. Anatomy only serves to build upon, but figures should never be made anatomical. Classic figures are constructed on the basis of outline. All youth and female figures should be represented by outline only. The celebrated *Apollo Belvedere* is an outline statue, the parts not being divided into muscular sections. Statues are interesting, either from their inherent beauty, or from their descriptive power. The ancients always paid the greatest attention to proportion and beauty of detail, the muscles never so predominating as to make one lose sight of the whole. Heroic statues, with the poetic element preponderating, do not depend so much for effect upon a nicety of proportion. Of this species are the works of Michael Angelo, which recommend themselves to the observer by an overpowering massiveness of detail. Proportion always follows the increase of size in a certain scale. The size of the feet is determined by the size of the head, which also governs the proportion of the whole body. A small head and small feet, with limbs pushed to the extreme of development, convey an idea of colossal strength; and, to attain this end, Michael Angelo knew precisely the value of a small head. The highest works of art are made for beauty alone, as the end and aim of expression. The Greeks never attained their highest perfection until they abandoned theological and descriptive art. Descriptive art existed in very early times. The Egyptians and Aztecs, knowing nothing of proportion, in common with other uncivilized nations, when they wished to represent great intellect, gave a number of heads to one figure; and great strength, in a similar manner, was indicated by numerous limbs.

C. A. N.

## V.

The lecture was chiefly occupied in the delineation and explanation of the muscles of the abdominal section, and of the back; and their opposite extremes of flexion and extension. There are more folds of the serratus muscle in classic statues than are found in life. The ancients had a conventional manner of representing some parts of the body. For example, they always made the opening of the ribs circular, though it is rarely found thus in life. These muscles have very little to do with proportion; but it is necessary to understand them in order to appreciate the highest beauties of ancient art, for the great excellence of those works rests in part upon the careful attention to these points. The superiority of the antique over modern art is proved by a comparison of the works of Michael Angelo with those of the ancients. Winckelmann accuses him of originating and promoting corruption of taste in sculpture, and cites his rilievo of *Apollo Flaying Marsyas* as being the very reverse of good taste. The same author says of the antique statue of *Niobe*, that it is " beautiful according to the highest conceptions of beauty." This comparison is suggested, not to disparage Michael Angelo, but to indicate his proper rank in art. Knowledge in this department is of little value to the man who proposes to make money out of art, who studies design with a view to printing calico, or some such end; but it is of the greatest use to the artist.

Referring to the human skeleton, by means of which the lecturer makes his statements clear, we observe the great projection of the spinous processes, which, at first glance it would appear, must be very prominent in the body. A transverse section of the body was drawn, showing how the spinous process is buried in a great mass of muscle outside. In apes, however much they may approach man, the ligament of the trochanter is wanting, a fact which might grieve a Darwinian. Broad, muscular shoulders are always associated with narrow flanks; and when the shoulders are flat and weak, there is a correspondingly increased development of the hips.

A drawing was made of a highly-celebrated work by Lysippus, *Apoxyomenes*, an athlete who is depicted scraping from himself with an iron the dust of Palæstra. A copy of it is now in the Vatican, displaying the delicate elasticity and graceful suppleness of a beautiful youthful figure of great perfection of form. A sketch was also given of the statue of *Illissus*, a river-god, the remains of which form one of the collection of Elgin Marbles. This is one of the finest antiques, having very little that is conventional about it; its great beauty consisting in its truth to nature.

C. A. N.

## VI.

Continuing the subject of the muscles of the body, we learn that the serratus is the artistic muscle of the side. The artists of the *Laocoön* — there were three of them — had no conception of the serratus muscle, so elegantly marked in the statue of the *Fighting Gladiator*. The serratus contracts, and brings the scapula forward, when a heavy weight is lifted at arm's-length. Common and classic forms were compared by means of drawings. In the common fine form, there is no separation of local sections, as in the classic form; and in common art there is an indefinite breaking-up of the surface, without regard to expression. Canova and others multiplied such forms in unlimited numbers. Canova's statue of *Hercules Throwing Lychas* gives occasion for such masking, but the effect is confused and unmeaning. The pectoral section is smooth, except in statues of Hercules. There is always a cavity where the ensiform cartilage occurs. There were two antique statues of Hercules, the *Farnesian* and the *Torso*, the latter of which represents the disembodied Hercules. The former is called the *Vulgar Hercules;* the parts seeming to be thrown together without any regard for their quality, only vastly over-powering the head by their size. The *Atlas*, a statue supporting a globe on its shoulders, is the worst statue of antiquity. In the *Torso*, the relation of the chest to the body is beautifully proportioned, and also in the *Venus de Milo*.

Representations of the Crucifixion with the head erect are erroneous in point of fact. The weight of the body being suspended from the arms, the head must be thrown forward, and buried within the deltoid muscles. In case of long-continued tension, the muscles are exhausted, becoming straight and flat, and losing all power of contraction. When they are in this state, they do not respond to the will.

The best proportions of the masculine form are obtained by enhancing to the greatest possible extent all male peculiarities. The greatest difference between modern and classic art is, that in the former the peculiarities are not emphasized. Crawford's statue of *Orpheus* is one of the worst examples of modern art. Ward's statue of an Indian is literally an Indian, and nothing more. Works like this individualize, and not generalize. In art we want the highest ideal generalizations, and our interest declines when individual peculiarities are given instead. This, of course, applies to high art, and not to portraiture.

Female proportion differs mainly in the size of the chest, which is smaller than in the male. The *Venus de Milo* is the best example for study of female proportion.

C. A. N.

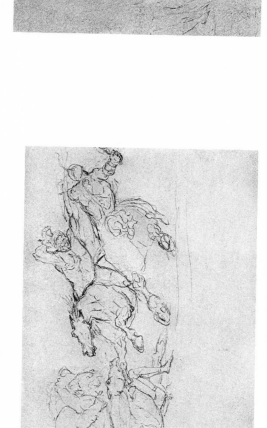

35. AND SATAN CAME ALSO

36. AND SATAN CAME ALSO

37. AND SATAN CAME ALSO

38. CUPID RELATING HIS ADVENTURES TO VENUS

## VII.

The subject under consideration was the anatomical construction of the thigh and pelvis with their appropriate muscles. The femur was drawn; showing the head, neck, shaft, condyles, and greater and less trochanters. The tensor of the femoral fascia in life has little expression; but in classic statues it gives rise to a peculiar, characteristic style of marking. The inner ankle is determined by the tibia, and is situated higher than the outer ankle: the latter is formed by the lengthening out of the fibula. The various muscles of the limbs were given, with their rise and insertion. We learn that the vastus internus muscle being attached to the upper part and inner side of the patella, gives a certain torsion to the limb, a feature much exaggerated by some sculptors; The knee is one of the most difficult parts of the human body to be represented in art, nothing requiring more care than the distribution of parts in this section. No work of art can be fine unless the articulations are well rendered. All the classic statues are distinguished by their fine knees and elbows, fine wrists and ankles.

The sartorius muscle was described as the longest of the human body. It is flat and slender, from an inch and a half to two inches in breadth. It arises by a tendon from the anterior superior spinous process of the ilium, extends obliquely inward over the rectus and vastus internus, and then, running down between the tendons of the adductor magnus and the gracilis, is inserted by a tendon into the inner part of the tibia. This muscle serves to bend the leg obliquely inward, or to roll the thigh outward, and at the same time to bring one leg across the other, on which account it received the name of *sartorius*, or the tailor's muscle.

C. A. N.

## VIII.

The time was chiefly occupied in the drawing of full-length figures, illustrating the general relation of the parts before considered ·in detail. These drawings, representing the human figure in various attitudes, displaying a minute anatomical knowledge, no less than perfect mastery of the mysteries of *foreshortening*, were the most interesting, as well as the most difficult of execution, of any in the whole course. In one drawing, when the figure was represented with the arms extended, and one knee flexed, the lecturer stated that he had marked the tensor of the femoral fascia, after the peculiar style of the antique, — that the classic statues are idealized, so that they are never like life. The local sections are individualized on an anatomical basis; and what would be the finest possible realization of form seems to have been universally agreed upon and accepted, so that in this respect the classic statues might all have been made by one person.

The serratus muscle is the least variable of any part of the muscular system. Had the artist studied the *Laocoön* from life, the muscles must have been more correctly represented.

C. A. N.

## IX.

The subject of the ninth lecture was the anatomical structure of the foot. The foot really is the hand adapted for walking, and has all the peculiarities of the hand. The great toe has two bones like the thumb, the other toes having three bones like the fingers. The front of the foot comprises the tarsal and metatarsal sections, and the phalanges. The second toe is longer usually than the others, and should always be thus represented in drawing an ideal foot. The muscles acting upon the foot, the tibialis anticus, the extensor proprius pollicis, and the peroneus, with its three divisions, although we see them but as a single muscle, were described with appropriate illustrations. The gastrocnemius and soleus muscles, forming the calf of the leg, unite to form the tendo achilles, the tendon of the heel. The arch of the foot has no support except the fascia, extending along the lower surface of the foot. To draw a foot properly, the muscular sections should be indicated. The inner and outer views of the foot and leg are very different. The inner ankle is higher than the outer; and, the higher the inner ankle, the higher the instep of necessity. Sometimes the instep is so high that water will run under the arch without wetting the sole of the foot, though we are forced to believe such instances are very rare.

In drawing the ankle the parts require the nicest adjustment, because the slightest inaccuracy destroys the proportion.

A drawing was made of a foreshortened foot, — the celebrated foot of Peter in Raphael's well-known painting of the *Transfiguration*. This is justly celebrated as an example of difficult drawing. The foot is extended towards the observer, showing the upper and lower surfaces at the same time.

C. A. N.

## X.

The subject of the lecture was foreshortening. In making foreshortened drawings, the artist has principally to depend on the prominences of the subject, and the perspective arrangements of parts.

If we wish to represent the body foreshortened, it is necessary to observe the relative proportions of the parts: for instance, in a side view of the body extended on the ground, we see the toes rise as high as the chest, and, noting all the prominences in this manner, mark them accordingly in our drawing. To obtain a foreshortened view of the face, a profile was sketched, having the chin considerably elevated; then horizontal lines were drawn from each feature, these lines representing the planes of the face, and the spaces between measuring the limits which each feature would occupy in a front view of the same elevation. The lecturer then drew within the spaces a foreshortened full face, which might be supposed to represent the same head before given in profile. This was the only plan, as far as the lecturer knew, by which foreshortening may be calculated; but to practise it requires some knowledge of form, an acquaintance with the details occurring in the subject, and a general idea of the whole proportion. With this preparation, after working out the problem, it will become apparent with practice what is needful to be done.

There are two methods of foreshortening, — by obscuration, the hiding of one part behind another, and by position, showing the perspective arrangements of parts. Almost every great artist has made attempts in foreshortening, the most difficult art in the world. The *Dead Christ*, by Raphael, is an instance. The *Last Judgment*, by Michael Angelo, contains many examples. The figures of Michael Angelo are peculiar in their massiveness and grand repose. In his reclining figures he makes the parts appear as if they had weight, by the way in which they rest upon the ground. Fine drawings were made, illustrating various points in the lecture. One portrayed an infant on his couch; another might represent Abel, after Cain had murdered him. Not the least attractive sketch was one of a cherub, reclining in mid-air, with a butterfly hovering over him.

The lecturer remarked, in conclusion, that this course covered only the simplest elements of design. To a knowledge of form, the painter must add information regarding the manners and customs of different periods, if he would paint a historical picture. He must know how to place an army, and how to represent a warrior. Persians, Greeks, and Romans must be very differently represented. Attention must also be paid to perspective, which causes parts to appear diminished in proportion to the distance.

C. A. N.

## XI.

The subject of the eleventh lecture was facial expression. There are two varieties of expression, — expression proper, which depends upon the anatomical structure, and what we call tension in expression, which is occasioned by the features in action. The study of expression is not the study of the mere form of the lines, but of the character and governing motives. Every face has an individual motive, — aggressive, secretive, retiring, or whatever it may be. Greater or less size also influences expression. All artistic races have concave faces. The type drawn represented the French, Irish, and Celtic races generally. The aggressive or conquering races have convex faces, retreating foreheads, Roman noses, and prominent chins, as the English, old Roman, and the majority of Americans. The eyebrows are raised, and the eyes very full. These peculiarities mark the permanently conquering races everywhere. The artistic races give tone to fashion, and predominate in matters of taste, just as the conquering English race predominates in other respects. The classic Greek profile was drawn, with the nose and forehead marked by a single straight line, the eyebrow straight and very close to the eye, the chin full and not prominent, the very worst type of chin, in the lecturer's opinion. This is the style of face characterizing all the classic statues, and is used alike to represent Venus and Juno, Jupiter and Apollo. The faces considered represent types, and are without tension. To whatever type a face may belong, its habitual expression indicates, in a great measure, its character. The lecturer then, from the various types, drew individual heads retaining all the characteristics, yet marked by various motives, — distrust, alertness, or self-confidence.

In some faces the expression is good, while the anatomical structure is of a low order. Persons with these faces often exhibit the greatest faithfulness and heroism, without intellectual ability, and are sometimes found among mechanics and negroes. There is a certain form of face peculiar to the French and Italians, and belonging to the very worst type. The structure of the face is animal; but all the lines of expression are intellectual and emotional, and the character such a face represents is fickle, insincere, artistic, — in short, Mephistopheles. The most indispensable requisite of a fine face is a direct, honest expression. We must be assured of the genuineness in order to fully appreciate the beauty of a face.

In drawing faces, we decide upon the type requisite for the subject, and proceed to individualize. The lecturer then showed how readily the typical English aggressive face might be modified so as to become the typical face of the English royal family, and of the old Bourbon house of Spain, presenting, in fact, a very good portrait of Queen Victoria. The nose is a very important feature; and by changing Victoria's aristocratic Roman nose for a concave, or even a straight one, we see how much the face loses in dignity. The next most important part is the chin. An otherwise fine face may be marred by a retreating chin, or an insignificant upper face redeemed by one firm and well-shaped.

In expression, one finds the result of temperament, intelligence, and emotion, not dependent on the anatomical structure. As it is common to find faithfulness and integrity in a certain low order of anatomical structure, it is no less unfrequent to find fine features spoiled by the habitual expression. The drawing illustrating this point might respectively represent Uncle Tom and Xantippe.

It is difficult to decide what makes the most beautiful head. The junction of the nose and forehead forms a most expressive part of the face. Yet the ancients in their statues merged this into one straight line. Not one person in twenty thousand has that peculiar formation, and we must regard it as a mere artistic expedient. We know that the ancients had types as various as our own.

The head of Julius Cæsar looks like an Americanized Scotchman, and that of Socrates like an Irishman.

Faces may have a whole expression which is harmonious, yet with the separate features out of balance.

The intention of the artist should be indicated by the action of the body, keeping the face placid. In this respect the classic artists were very much in advance of those of our own times. The lecturer illustrated this point by sketching a face with no action, and showed, by adding to it a body in action, how it assumed an expression to suit the action. The expression is latent in the face; which the lecturer proved by sketching a body requiring the most opposite expression, which the face seemed at once to assume. We associate expression with action. In short, we learn in art, the less done to the face the better; and the artist should above all things be careful not to exaggerate.

The Greeks used head-dresses conforming to the shape of the head, displaying the contour. The opposite practice seems to prevail at this day. The more finely shaped the head, the more difficult to add any thing in the way of adornment. Every thing worn on the head becomes a part of it, and contributes to the general expression. The very ponderous head-dress enlarges the head to such an extent as to destroy the symmetry of the whole figure.

In conclusion, the lecturer observed that expression was an inexhaustible subject; that the various topics he had mentioned were only introductory titles to volumes which might be written about it.

C. A. N.

## XII.

The subject of this lecture was infantile proportion. The differences between the adult and the child were pointed out. Attention was called to the greater height of the head above the ear, the long body, flat shoulders, short limbs, and integumentary masses, in the child. The spinal column in man is erect and curved, in woman less curved and inclined forward, and in children nearly straight and still more inclined forward. Comparing a transverse section of the chest, we find it oval in man, more circular in woman, and nearly round in children. The body of an adult man is erect, and the shoulders should be directly over the outer ankle. The body of a woman is inclined forward, and it is impossible from her structure for her to stand perfectly erect. In children and women the cerebral section is larger than the facial.

The drawings given by Dr. Rimmer of children were exceedingly spirited and graceful. Three cherubs floating in the air were marvels of grace; and, indeed, every one was remarkable for its graphic representation of the characteristics of infancy.

C. A. N.

It was a common regret with Dr. Rimmer's pupils that his blackboard-drawings could not be preserved. It is also to be regretted that his lectures in Boston, or at the Cooper Institute, could not have been reported *verbatim*. They would have made a book of priceless value, and of its kind unique. A lady artist, who attended the Providence and Cooper Institute lectures, says, that " the latter contained more detail; the former were reported for two reasons, — first, to give the entertaining side of the doctor's art lore; and, second, in the hope of inspiring a public interest that should result in something permanent. He always assigned a high place to women in the scale of creation, quite in contrast to the assertion of Miss Hardaker, in the July number of 'The North American Review' for 1880, that women are hopelessly inferior, as a rule, in physical strength and brain-power, to men; but the doctor was always gallant and loyal to our sex, believing and expecting the highest achievements from it."

39. DYING CENTAUR

# CHAPTER XIII.

## RIMMER AND HUNT.

### 1870-1879.

R. RIMMER was particularly interested in art education after he came to Boston in 1861, and thought seriously in what way a broad, well-founded, and thorough art-school might be established. He was especially impressed with the necessity of free classes, where genius without money could enjoy the advantages of the best instruction. He believed from his own experience, and was confirmed in the opinion by observation, that artists come generally from the lower classes, and that it is the high duty of the State to undertake their instruction.

William M. Hunt, who had settled to Boston in 1862, was occupied also with plans for a free school of art; and he at length proposed to Dr. Rimmer that together they should open such an institution, each giving instruction in whatever branches he felt his attainments best suited. Of this proposal, however, nothing came.

After the sculptor's return from New York in 1870, Mr. Hunt renewed his proposal; but the former did not feel hopeful of its success, although Mr. Hunt urged his plan with his characteristic vigor and earnestness, arguing, that, should they once begin, the State would give them aid, and they would certainly be enabled to continue an enterprise that would result in lasting public good. Even this prospect did not arouse Dr. Rimmer's enthusiasm: his experience did not buoy up his hope, though he was naturally disposed to join in the project. Beyond Mr. Hunt's ardent words nothing resulted, and the affair was soon forgotten.

Both men had instructed female pupils almost exclusively, and they were fully alive to the prospective significance of the art disposition as manifested to such a surprising extent by the sex in this country. Dr. Rimmer would sometimes remark, half reprovingly, when one of his pupils married, " When you get so that you can do something, you marry." Mr. Hunt observed upon one occasion, that, were he asked to select six of the most talented young artists in Boston, he should be obliged to choose from the women.

During the winters of 1869–70 and 1870–71, Mr. Hunt taught a large class of women in drawing and painting. He felt the necessity of awakening the community to the value of art and its influences, and he thought that he could do something to that end by appealing to the sensibilities and quickness of perception of women. The response was ready and appreciative, the master and pupils entering into the work with great energy and perseverance. Teaching under certain conditions would have been a continuous charm to him. He recognized its value, and understood the necessity of mental contact with young, studious minds. He gave up the charge of the school to one of his pupils in 1871–72, though visiting it regularly.

It was unfortunate for the public good that two artists like Rimmer and Hunt could not have been identified with some distinctive project of art education. From 1861 until the year of their deaths (1879), these men were the principal art elements of Boston. Each admired the other, and their personal relations were very friendly. Dr. Rimmer posed for the hands in Hunt's large portrait of Lincoln, which was burned in the great fire in Boston. In their profession they had little in common. Their temperaments, art-spheres, and lives were as different as could well be. Their methods of teaching conducted the pupil through different paths, with the intention of arriving at the same goal. Rimmer taught that the constructive character of an object was the first thing to learn, and the acquisition of knowledge of the first importance, as the only means of expressing an art sentiment or idea correctly and successfully.

The teaching of Hunt made the expression of the essential quality of an object as an artistic effect of the first importance, with the understanding that the knowledge of art, anatomy, perspective, ethnology, and the rest would follow in the pupil's progress as a conscious necessity. It was a direct appeal to the art-instinct, and a confidence in the intuitive sense. Rimmer admired nature as a fact to be made subservient to the imagination; Hunt, as a sympathy to respond to. Rimmer used a figure or landscape as a constructive principle to express the idea of his mind; Hunt used them as individualities, as suggesters. The latter believed that the joyous exercise of the fancy, a sensibility to the influence of every living thing and to every work of art, were the prime conditions of the artist; and that art -education should be based solely on the great and solemn pleasure of developing these qualities. Methods and systems he despised: he trusted to the nature of the pupil. Rimmer taught all students the same course of study, — to know nature, but to rely upon knowledge and imagination in the execution of a work. Nature, nor men, nor women, inspired him to any effort or expression.

When Hunt was considering the proposition that had been made to him to undertake the decoration of two large stone panels in the Assembly Chamber of the New-York State Capitol at Albany, he thought that if he could secure the assistance of Dr. Rimmer and Mr. J. P. Rinn, — an architect and decorator of Boston, whose talents he much admired, — he should be able to finish the work in the required time; and he anticipated much pleasure in their all working together.

Mr. Hunt visited Dr. Rimmer at his house on several occasions, to consult about the advisability of undertaking the work, and to arrange upon some plan by which they could aid each other in its execution. He invited the doctor to visit his studio, look over his sketches of the proposed paintings, and criticise them. He also gave the doctor a charcoal-sketch of the *Discoverer*, — one of the proposed pictures, — so that the latter could consider it as a composition, and make suggestions at his leisure. The doctor made a sketch of the subject, according to his own idea of how it should be treated, which is extremely interesting, as showing how easily the slightest human professional relation or influence disturbed him. After he had made the sketch, he abandoned the idea of even thinking of Hunt's compositions, and told the latter that all he could do for him was simply to reproduce the designs after their composition had been definitely decided upon.

Beside the subjects that were painted in the Capitol, Hunt had in consideration quite a series, embracing the principal elements of the character of the State, treated symbolically. One of these he described to the doctor, and the latter made a pencil-sketch of it. A grand composition it is, though resembling a classic, rather than a modern, way of illustrative thinking. While Hunt was executing the work in Albany, he described to me in detail quite a number of the above-mentioned series of pictures. Nothing that I had ever read or seen exceeded his brilliant, individual, and comprehensive ideas.

It is a common assertion that Hunt was not an original or imaginative artist. He was not in the same sense that Rimmer was; but he had a perception as clear and correct, an understanding as true, and a capacity of utilizing his powers as certain, as any artist of his time. The pleasure of expressing his impressions of an individual or of nature was stronger than his imaginative fertility; but these qualities always worked together in his best circumstanced efforts.

His portraits possess very high qualities of imaginative consideration. When the occasion came, in conversation with some artist-friend, he gave the most surprising proofs of a fertility of subject, of grand and individual style of treating them, and of a most loyal recognition of the propriety of locality in their expression. Hunt lived in his day and generation, but without that recognition which was absolutely necessary for the exercise of his best possibilities.

Rimmer had nothing to do with the influences about him. He lived on the high mountain of imagination, and enjoyed the locality for himself alone.

As might have been expected by those who knew the two men, the moment they came into working, professional intercourse, there was an irreconcilable difference. Dr. Rimmer's criticisms did not please Hunt; and the latter's detailed scheme of their working together was any thing but satisfactory to the former. The artists parted with the conviction that there could be no community of art-work between them. For the time that Dr. Rimmer spent in these conferences and visits, Mr. Hunt paid him one hundred dollars.

A wealthy citizen of Boston proposed at one time to establish a school for the design of textile fabrics, and asked Dr. Rimmer's opinion regarding such a scheme. The following letter was written in reply, and was accompanied by several pages of foolscap-paper covered with pencil-drawings of a large variety of plants and flowers. The death of the person principally interested ended further consideration of the matter.

## LETTER FROM DR. RIMMER ON DESIGN OF TEXTILE FABRICS.

Mr. —— ——.

Allow me to suggest that the great difficulty with us in the way of making designs for textile fabrics, which would be acceptable to persons of taste, is a want of knowledge of the elementary principles and forms to be employed for the purpose. No person, however talented, can be expected to design a flower or fruit piece who is ignorant of the form of fruit and flowers; for, as a beautiful whole is made up of a collection or variety of beautiful parts, beautiful in themselves, or held so by comparison, the whole can only be made beautiful by a knowledge of what is individually beautiful, or what is made to appear so by judicious contrasts. Complete designs, like sentences, though

40.   THE DISCOVERER

41.   THE FLIGHT OF NIGHT

infinite in variety, are nevertheless made up of a limited number of parts, as words are composed of single letters, and language made up of simple sounds; and these parts are the natural objects with which the designer has to deal. Upon this point there is so excellent an opportunity to say too much, for any purpose short of an exhaustive treatise, upon things proper to be used in ornamental art, that, fearing myself, I will say no more than is necessary to point in brief to the natural divisions of things and methods presenting themselves for consideration.

The forms most used in design for textile fabrics are those of flowers, leaves, twigs, grasses, shrubs; also straight, curved, and angular lines, architectural vines and flourishes, vases, urns, birds and insects, crystalline and kaleidoscopic forms, waves, clouds, etc.

To be able to draw these well, they should be studied, one order at a time, each until it is well understood, beginning with the simplest and ending with the most complex; when the students would be prepared for the next step, which, I think, should be the study of colors. And here it might be well to begin with a comparison of the different shades of the same color in simple lines and cross lines.

Then a comparison of what might be called the primitives, — white, black, red, blue, and yellow; first two, then three, and so on through all the varieties of shade.

Then a comparison of the simple compounds, as white and black, red and yellow, yellow and blue, blue and red, and so on through all the secondary tints. Then there should be a study for the effect of colors at a distance and by candle-light; and this should be done until the eye was well trained to the perception of the tenderest beauties, when the pupil should be permitted to compose, adding color to form; painting leaves, flowers, crystals, birds, insects, etc.; after which composition in full should be attempted, which would be the uniting of all the forms with all the colors, in any way the student might devise. Here would be opened a new field in the effect of different colors with hard linen, cotton with woollen, transparent and semi-transparent gauzes, with opaque cottons, and felts, for which purpose the student should have the proper material at hand. The last step would be to study how to apply colors to objects in such a way as to have them distinct enough to be transferred or copied upon different blocks for the purpose of printing, and at the same time so as to preserve, when printed, their tenderness and delicacy of mingling.

This, in brief, is the plan I would adopt for the formation of a school of design for designers for textile fabrics; and though it would be a work of considerable labor to make example-boards or sketches for the use of the pupils, and a heavy task to oversee, illustrate, and direct their efforts to proper ends, yet, if once established, and in successful operation for a sufficient length of time, I doubt not you would have gained an advantage there never could be lost.

Very respectfully,

W. RIMMER.

October, 1864.

# CHAPTER XIV.

## BOOKS AND VARIOUS PROJECTS.

### 1864-1874.

A an early age Dr. Rimmer manifested a fondness for literary composition, and formed the habit of prose and poetical writing which he continued through life. Many of his early productions were profusely illustrated with fine pencil-drawings. Several illustrations of a poem written when he was fourteen years of age, and called "The Midnight Ride," are still preserved, although too much defaced for reproduction. One of them, with much difficulty traced by his daughter, Miss C. H. Rimmer, is given to show how the boy's mind was at that age peopled with hobgoblins and other frightful creatures. It also illustrates his disposition to make very finely-finished drawings. In later years he carried this tendency so far as to execute them by the aid of a microscope.

His writings, like the majority of his drawings and sketches in clay, were simply sketched out sufficiently to define the idea embodied. One long and elaborate poem, written at various times during his life, and partly illustrated, is entitled "Stephen and Philip." Its plan embraces a consideration of terrestrial and celestial experiences, principles, beliefs, and hopes. He also made lengthy comments on Darwin's writings. It is the intention of Miss C. H. Rimmer to prepare all of her father's literary productions for publication.

In 1864 Dr. Rimmer published his "Elements of Design." The work was in six parts, with forty-nine steel-plate illustrations and forty-two pages of text. It was intended to be an aid to teachers and parents in instructing children; and so great is its merit that it should be authorized by statute as the universal text-book of the country.

The first lesson begins in the simplest way, and by means of straight lines only, to illustrate the movement of the human figure. In this lesson the author shows that he understood the first principle which should be taught to an art-student; to wit, that the general movement of the human figure is the first thing which a pupil must understand, and that all movement proceeds, and is governed, from the centre. It is not only eminently true in place and kind for a beginner, but it is valuable also to artists. The lessons go on by easy steps to the complete construction of a figure at rest or performing some function. From simple lines the author proceeds to mark the divisions and proportions of the body, and finally to indicate its anatomical character. The lessons include studies in types, expressions, and draperies.

Dr. Rimmer contemplated publishing another and still more amusing work, with the title of "The Baby Drawing Book," especially adapted for children, wherein he proposed treating every living object that the child first sees, as domestic and other animals, in the same primary way that he had the human form in "The Elements of Design." Nothing could have been more sensible, charming, and intelligent. The plan was, however, given up, there being really no encouragement for any thing of the kind. The stupendous mass of rubbish sold in the United States under the name of "drawing-books" and similar titles, for the purpose of teaching the young to draw, has quite supplied the market.

In 1877 the artist published what in some respects was the most important work he ever executed, — his "Art Anatomy."

The book owes its existence to the generous thought of Mrs. W. A. Tappan, a Boston lady, who desired in some way to secure a permanent expression of the knowledge which Dr. Rimmer had for so many years displayed upon the lecture-platform. His own preference was to make a statue: but it was finally concluded that a book would be the best form for the work; and Mrs. Tappan deposited the sum of two thousand dollars in the hands of Mr. Edward W. Hooper, treasurer of Harvard University, to pay for the publication of such a book on this subject as Dr. Rimmer should prepare.

The work contains eighty pages full of illustrations, reproduced by the heliotype process, in red ink from pencil-drawings, nearly all of which the doctor made during the summer vacation of 1876, spent in Union, N. H. The heliotype plate is ten by fourteen inches in size; and the book contains nearly nine hundred drawings, illustrating in the fullest manner the ethnological, bony, anatomical, and artistic construction, movement (both simple and composite), and purposes of the human form, of both sexes and all ages, as well as the expression of the passions, with full explanatory text on the same page with the drawings.

The drawings are for the most part in outline, and are made with great firmness and beauty. Many of the figures are statues in their conception. There is one full-page composition entitled the *Call to Arms*. The "Art Anatomy" is the most perfect compendium of pictorial and artistic knowledge on this subject that I have ever seen, and is without doubt unique. It is more interesting, however, to the learned than to beginners, — a work of art, not a student's text-book. It confirms what has often been said of its author, "He talked higher than the heads of his hearers."

Many of the heads in the "Art Anatomy" were taken from life with almost photographic precision; and many of them are easily recognized. The book gives a partial idea of the power of the author in seizing a distinctive likeness, and of the rapidity and exactness with which he worked. The original drawings were made at first stroke, being very seldom retouched.

Fifty copies of the work were published; and a few over half have been sold at fifty dollars each. One might suppose that such a work would at least have found a place at once in every public library in the land, as well as in many private ones. The only pecuniary return received by the author was the profits on the sales. While he believed that the book would meet a present need, he by no means regarded it as a full expression of his knowledge on the subject of which it treated. Its production was in every way an agreeable task. The doctor often remarked, "Anatomy is the only subject."

The study of anatomy by the artist is at once a pleasure and a pain, — a pleasure, because it helps him to express himself more clearly and easily than he otherwise could; a pain, because all books on the subject lack the very thing which he wants, — the clearest and quickest method to construct a figure. If Dr. Rimmer had made a work on anatomy for artists on the simple, primitive principle upon which he wrote his "Elements of Design," he would have won the unfailing gratitude of generations of artists. Had he laid upon the skeleton the muscles as they should be placed in building up a figure, without reference to any division, section, or composite arrangement, he would have satisfied a need which every young artist feels. Given the skeleton, to teach the first muscle, then the second, the third, and so on, until the entire figure is constructed: is the primary, all-important programme of an anatomy for artists. After this, the more intimate and profound knowledge of the subject may follow in its proper order, as required by the artist. At one time Dr. Rimmer began the compilation of a book of questions and answers for the study of anatomy, as wide and thorough in its extent as was his knowledge of that subject. It is to be seriously regretted that it never was completed. The truth is, that there was so little demand for any thing which the doctor could do of this kind, that he did not feel encouraged to complete a work of such magnitude.

When in New York, Dr. Rimmer and Mr. W. J. Linton, the wood-engraver, considered together the project of an elaborate work on art anatomy. The latter was especially desirous of assisting in such an undertaking, and offered to do the engraving, and take the chances of sale in return for his labor.

In March, 1875, Mr. Joseph Billings, a Boston architect, contracted with Dr. Rimmer to make a model in plaster of a statue of *Faith*, nine feet high, from which was to be cut one thirty-six feet high for the National Monument to the Forefathers at Plymouth, Mass.

The sculptor agreed to make this statue, and deliver it in plaster, in two and a half months from the date of the contract, for the sum of two thousand dollars. The contract stated that the figure was to be made " after the design of the late Hammatt Billings " (the architect of the monument), and " be done to the entire satisfaction and acceptance of Mr. Joseph Billings."

A small model of the original design was furnished the sculptor for his guidance.

After the figure had been completed in plaster, as represented in plate eight, by a reproduction of the original photograph taken by Mr. Billings without Dr. Rimmer's knowledge or consent, the former paid the sculptor the amount agreed upon, removed the statue, and placed it in charge of another sculptor to " use as a framework " upon which to make another figure which should be satisfactory to Mr. Billings. This sculptor succeeded in his task by making a new head, adding a large amount of drapery to the figure, and received for his labor the sum of three hundred dollars.

Dr. Rimmer accepted the price fixed by the contract, although far from satisfied with his work. From the beginning to the end of this transaction, there were differences of opinion and misunderstandings between himself and Mr. Billings in regard to the execution of the statue. The same differences exist to-day in the minds of those familiar with the circumstances, and I find it impossible to arrive at any satisfactory basis for further observations.

The most curious incident in Dr. Rimmer's art life was his connection with the project of the American Photo-Sculpture Company of New York. The prospectus prepared by him for the company is still more curious, as a description of an enterprise with which, of all men or artists, one would suppose Dr. Rimmer would have been the last to identify himself.

The managers of this concern seemed to repose great confidence in their prospective success, if they could secure Dr. Rimmer's name and assistance; and he entertained a like conviction.  He was expected to add the art to the completed mechanical part, and thus give an artistic character to a work commenced with a machine.  It is unnecessary to go into a lengthy explanation of the doubtful character, so far as art is concerned, of this scheme.  It is enough to say, that it never had any repute in the estimation of good sculptors nor of the art world.  It had a practical existence in Paris, as a commercial project solely; and its continued existence depended upon the innocent and pretentious ignorance of the army of shoddy tourists who annually visit that capital.  The commonest workmen in clay were the artists who added the art to photo-sculpture in that city; no higher grade of artists condescending to have any thing to do with it.  What induced a man of the sensibility, professional pride, and perception of Dr. Rimmer, to identify himself with such a scheme, it is difficult to explain, unless it was done in one of those moments when the urgent need of a larger income appeared imperative.  The pecuniary inducements offered to him were one-tenth of the profits, and two thousand dollars' worth of stock.  Fortunately for the fame of Dr. Rimmer, nothing ever came of this company.

Many of the sculptor's friends desired that he might visit Europe.  One lady offered to defray his expenses, but he declined to accept any assistance which he felt would embarrass him with obligations; and under no circumstances did he wish to go, unless he could be accompanied by his family, which consisted of his wife and three daughters.  Concerning the possible results of such a visit his youngest daughter remarks, —

" If father had gone to Europe, I do not think he would have followed the tide of fashion, but would have selected some place in Italy, Spain, or Greece, and settled down to quiet study.  I think he expected eventually to see these countries.  Under proper circumstances he would have started at any moment.  The phenomena of light in Norway and Sweden and other northern latitudes was a subject upon which he often conversed.  I am not sure that he would ever have met the great artists abroad; for the reason that he would have been obliged to introduce himself as one entitled to recognition, and this I think he would never have been willing to do.  To present a letter of introduction was for him an impossibility.  He admired men for the noble acts they did, more than for a personal acquaintance.  It was a source of positive pleasure to him to think and to talk of brave lives and self-sacrifice."

43. FIGURES

We have seen that in his early life Rimmer entered into many schemes which promised greater pecuniary returns than the pursuit of art. In 1874 he fancied that a large public aquarium would not only be a good investment, but serve also a good educational purpose; and he accordingly hired rooms on Tremont Street, and began to fit them up with the necessary appliances. Many people thought that such a place of entertainment was a public necessity, and could be made to yield a handsome profit. Just before the tanks were ready to receive their intended inhabitants, the doctor became convinced that the enterprise could not be a success; and he abandoned it, losing all that he had invested in it, a sum amounting to several thousand dollars.

Another form in which his desire for money showed itself was a constant attempt to hit upon some profitable invention. At one time he had made some improvement in a gun-lock; at another, some self-registering plan to determine the number of persons entering a street-car; still, again, his plan was the construction in a cheap and durable material of a peculiar form of trunk, convenient for use and handling, and, as he used to say, "such as no expressman could break." But all these, as well as numberless other plans, came in the end to nothing but vague hopes and words.

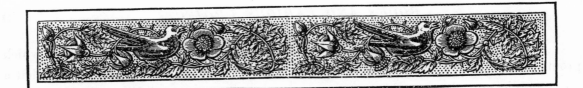

# CHAPTER XV.

## BOSTON ART MUSEUM.

### 1877–1879.

HEN the School of Drawing and Painting was opened in the autumn of 1876, in the Museum of Fine Arts in Boston, Dr. Rimmer was engaged to take charge of the instruction in anatomy. He began his first course of lectures in January, 1877, — in one of the rooms of the Institute of Technology, as those in the Museum were not ready, — and closed in the month of June.

The course consisted of two lectures a week, of an hour each, for which he received one thousand dollars. On the first day's lecture the doctor drew exercises on the blackboard; and the second the same exercises were drawn by the students, and were criticised by him and them.

The second school-year began Oct. 1, 1877, and closed the middle of the following June, including a vacation of two weeks. The lectures were given as before in the Institute of Technology.

During the third school-year Dr. Rimmer occupied rooms in the Museum building, adding to his duties as a lecturer, that of instruction in anatomical modelling, to which he gave two mornings of each week, his salary for this year being two thousand dollars.

The doctor found it somewhat difficult to quickly fall into the plans of the school directors. At his age, and after his experience of independent action, conforming to the regulations of others was both onerous and annoying.

The following correspondence on this subject explains itself, and gives the doctor's ideas of how his department of an art school should be conducted.

90

## COL. CABOT TO DR. RIMMER.

BOSTON, Feb. 14, 1877.

MY DEAR SIR, — I am sorry that it has not been in my power to attend some of your lectures since the first; and, from what I learn, I fear you have not fully understood the intention of the committee in regard to them. It was, that they should be strictly confined to anatomy as it concerns art. The lecture I heard seemed to me admirable, as it showed so clearly what no one understands so well as you, — the proportion which one part of the structure of the head, as relating to another, affects expression. Any time given to the general subject of shading or composition would be repeating what is taught in the other departments of the school, where the appliances are more suitable, and, I fear, would mar the completeness of your course. As we, by the light of the experience already had, can now judge more exactly what is wanted, would it not be well to draw up an exact syllabus of the course, so that students could prepare, in a measure, beforehand for what was coming? This mode of systematic procedure would, I think, in the end be more satisfactory to you as well as the committee.

Ever sincerely,

EDWARD C. CABOT.

## DR. RIMMER'S REPLY.

COL. CABOT.

*Dear Sir,* — I am glad I have received this last note; as it enables me, without obtruding myself upon your notice, to correct what seems to me to be a wrong impression touching my intentions.

Much as I desire the welfare of the whole school, and willing as I am to be under complete control, as an instructor working under a definitely arranged plan should, I have only given as much time as that assigned me in the programme. I have been at my post according to instruction, neither sooner nor later, and have given no other instruction than what fairly relates to art anatomy. I have avoided all reference to color, and even to light and shade, and have only accepted this class in sculpture, and the later review, in accordance with express instruction to that effect; though, to my mind, it is absolutely necessary that some such thing should be done by some one who is able to hold the student to his work upon purely æsthetic grounds. Still, this is not my concern. I am not director here, and by no means insist upon the adoption of my plan.

Sometimes, in fact often, the members of my class compel me to give them the last moment; and I am often requested to remain to impart some further information when I should be glad to be on my way home.

Consider, my dear sir, that it is not my fault if the pupils are willing to do their utmost for the acquisition of such knowledge as you have employed me to impart to them. The pupil feels himself already like a bird at large, soaring on his own wings when relying upon his instinct: I tell him to get up and make the attempt to fly. I beg your pardon for the use of this metaphor. . . .

I have kept away from the other departments to the extent of not even visiting them at all, or of speaking of them, and while I remain attached to the school shall continue to do so; this being, in my judgment, a course most likely to give to others what I should claim for myself, — a fair chance to carry out their own plans. In short, this which I am doing is one of my means of procuring a livelihood; and I wish and intend to make myself as useful, and to live as quiet a life, as some disappointment, much experience, and my age demand for me.

It will give me great pleasure to prepare the required programme, thanking you for the kindly spirit pervading your note.

I remain yours very truly,

W. RIMMER.

The following is the first draught of a letter sent to the chairman of the committee having charge of the Museum school, in reply to a request for a statement of Dr. Rimmer's plan of instruction: —

DEAR SIR, — In compliance with your request, I send you a statement in full of the course of instruction adopted in my department of the School of Fine Arts.

On Thursdays of every week the class meets at the lecture-room in the Institute of Technology, at half-past two o'clock, for instruction in art anatomy. For the first hour, the members of the class copy from the blackboard, into their books, such drawings and their accompanying explanations, and such figures in illustration of the points under consideration, as I have made for them for that purpose. The second hour is given to blackboard-exercise on the part of the class; the drawings of each pupil being, before the hour is ended, brought under the criticism of the whole class.

On Tuesdays the class meets for review of original drawings at half-past two o'clock. One hour is devoted to this subject, and the other to general instruction touching the subject in hand, and as the needs of the moment make necessary.

On Saturday it has been arranged for us that the sculpture class, just now organized in accordance with instructions to this effect, meets at the sculpture-room of the Art Museum school, at nine o'clock in the morning, for two hours' exercise and study; after which, in the lecture-room at the Institute of Technology, the next two hours are devoted to the members of the class individually for such instruction as each may need for himself.

In conclusion, I beg to say that the thing most needed in my department is a broad and liberal course of general instruction in art anatomy, and an opportunity on the side of the teacher to do whatever may be necessary to follow the bent of individual talent to its full development.          I remain, etc.,

W. RIMMER.

## DR. RIMMER TO PROFESSOR W. R. WARE.

DEAR SIR,—I should think it would be an improvement over the present method, if students in the department of art anatomy could devote their time mainly to that subject; that other studies, however necessary in their way, should be in practice, as they are in fact, of secondary importance to them.

That certain whole days, from morning till night, with every advantage for the study of his subject, for blackboard-drawing, drawing from life, the study of illustrative casts, and the practice of sculpture, should be given them; that they should have a roomy and well-lighted place for study; that this room may be open at all times to the members of the class; that every student should have his own blackboard and modelling-stand and stool; that, on the days above mentioned, the teacher should be constantly present with his pupils; that no pupil should be permitted to draw from life except in connection with the study of those elements of art anatomy which alone can make such drawings useful to him, or advance him in the study of the principles of his profession. The teacher should be required to approve the living model. The model should sit but once a week. That, until a pupil has passed successfully through one branch of his subject, he shall not be permitted to take up another; that the right of the teacher to exact from his pupils the requisite drill to enable them to master their subject shall be peremptory; that there shall be, as now, for every pupil who may choose to attend, one open lecture a week, with a review on the same day. I do not believe in permitting any pupil to slight the advantages offered here in this school; and I believe that, when the several elementary departments of instruction are classified and taught separately,—as they should be,—the school will be one of the best in the country. I believe in systematizing the course of instruction with regard to the advancing of principles, rather than for the adoption of any personal or technical method whatsoever. I am of the opinion that better results may be expected from a well-graded course of instruction, than from the personal excellences of any teacher whatever; that the methods of a great school should rest upon some better foundation than personal methods. I believe every department of art—still life, landscape, animal art anatomy, and human art anatomy—has each a set of principles of its own, worthy the elucidation of our very ablest men.

If we can begin rightly, aiming at the highest excellence in the method of instruction, simplify its greatest difficulties, explain its philosophy, and carry the pupil in an authorized way up to the highest principles of his profession, it will be much to the credit of all concerned; for such methods are what are very much needed. The school may have to wait some little time for recognition of its merits, but it will come in the end. . . .

I respectfully suggest the above improvements.

The effects of a life of extreme mental and physical labor were already very perceptibly diminishing Dr. Rimmer's strength, when he returned to Boston. It was only by the severest effort that he was enabled to continue his lectures at the Museum, although his courage and enthusiasm never abated.

Towards the end of the spring of 1879, his strength seemed suddenly to fail; and, a ten-days' vacation not proving of any appreciable service, he at last reluctantly yielded to the urgent representations of the authorities of the school and to the advice of his physician, and abandoned his classes six or eight weeks before the conclusion of his course. He thought that rest would soon rid him of the sense of overpowering fatigue which oppressed him, and was full of plans for preparing, during the summer, such diagrams illustrative of his next winter's work, as would serve to lighten the labor of perpetually drawing upon the blackboard, which he had begun to find severe. After a few weeks spent at his home in Chelsea, he went to pass the summer with a married daughter in South Milford, taking with him the great sheets of paper upon which his diagrams were to be drawn. These he never found strength even to begin upon. His extreme nervous prostration continued to increase, accompanied by great physical distress, until the night of the 20th of August, when he passed quietly away.

His remains were laid beside those of his children in the little cemetery at East Milton.

It had been the intention of the managers of the Museum school, that Dr. Rimmer should continue a member of the corps of teachers as long he lived. The third annual report of the trustees closes an appreciative notice of his death, with the following words : —

" It is a pleasure to believe, that, after many years of alternate success and disappointment, mainly spent in teaching anatomy in its relations to the fine arts, he at last found in this school, not only a safe and happy haven in a premature old age, but a field of usefulness and activity better suited to his capacities and temperament than any he had known. The regular occupation and the definite compensation thus assured to him relieved him from many uncertainties and anxieties ; while the number of his pupils, and the fact that they took, for the most part, a serious interest in their work, was naturally a source of the greatest satisfaction to him."

Dr. Rimmer had, in January, 1862, joined the Boston Art Club, and occasionally sent pictures to its exhibitions. He resigned his membership before leaving Boston in 1866, thinking himself unfairly treated in the rejection of some of his paintings, and

COURTESY, FOGG ART MUSEUM, HARVARD UNIVERSITY; GIFT OF MRS. HENRY SIMONDS.

45. VENUS AND CUPID

44. MADONNA

in the hanging of others. After his return from New York, he rejoined the club, and presented to it the plaster-group of the FIGHTING LIONS. After the meeting of the club which followed his death, the following resolution was offered by the president, Mr. C. C. Perkins, and adopted by the club as a tribute of respect to Dr. Rimmer's memory, and in recognition of the talents and important services he had rendered in advancing and elevating the cause of art education in Boston : —

" *Resolved*, That we, members of the Boston Art Club, feel the death of Dr. William Rimmer to be a most serious loss, both to us and to the community in which he lived. His profound knowledge of anatomy, coupled with his great artistic talent, fitted him to render the most important services to art education ; and we may long wait before we can hope to fill the place which he has left vacant."

In manhood and later life the personal appearance of Dr. Rimmer was distinguished and striking. He was a powerfully built man, his hand-shake being rather suggestive of a grip from the paw of a lion. His height was five feet and ten inches, his body being proportionally rather long ; his weight averaged one hundred and fifty-five pounds. He walked with a dignified stride, carrying, when on the street, a heavy walking-stick, which he generally held horizontally. A stranger was likely to infer from his mien that he was haughty and aristocratic, although this was far from the truth.

Politically he was a Republican during the civil war, and later on an Independent ; but he never took any active part in politics.

Among the poets, Dr. Rimmer's favorites were Shakespeare, Dante, Homer, Poe, and Burns ; " The Tempest " being the play of the first named which he preferred. Among composers he delighted most in Beethoven, of listening to whose music he was never weary ; and the music of the Catholic Church affected him deeply.

In religious matters he himself was bound by no church or creed, although he expected and desired that his children should attend public worship until old enough to form opinions of their own. He placed no denominational restrictions upon them. " Go," he said, " wherever the gospel of Christ is preached." He always rented a pew in whatever church his family desired to attend. His own religious views were high and noble. He had no respect for priestcraft for its own sake, but held a clergyman at what he was worth as a teacher by precept and example, and no more. He had a great love for the Bible, and Job was his ideal. He once remarked that it was always his desire to deal with Scriptural subjects in his work.

Nothing could shake his faith in Providence, and the government of the world by a divine Being; but this belief only came after long years of severe struggle and examination. His knowledge and understanding of the constructive character of things were at times in violent antagonism with his imagination. The ideal creations of the latter were not sufficient evidences of the reality of a spirit-world. The reconciliation of the religious part of his nature to those just mentioned formed an harmonious and perfect faith in a divine existence hereafter.

# CHAPTER XVI.

## EXHIBITION OF DR. RIMMER'S WORKS.

### 1880.

IN May, 1880, there was opened in the Museum of Fine Arts in Boston an exhibition of one hundred and forty-six specimens of Dr. Rimmer's paintings, drawings, and sculpture.

It was the first exhibition of the kind ever held in this country; and in art interest it has had but one rival, — the Hunt exhibition of the previous winter. The contrast shown in the lives of the two artists was still more strikingly manifested in the events following their deaths.

In many respects Hunt's art life was brilliantly successful, while Rimmer's was a continual disappointment. An extraordinary tribute was paid to Hunt's memory immediately after his death by an exhibition, in the Boston Art Museum, of three hundred and twenty-eight of the best examples of his work; charcoal and crayon drawings and several pieces of sculpture and cameo-cutting being included with the paintings. People visited the collection with uncovered heads, and conversed, if at all, in whispers. During its continuance more than twenty thousand dollars were subscribed to buy some of his pictures for the Museum; but the prices ranged so high when these were sold, that it was deemed inadvisable to make any purchases, and the money was returned to the subscribers. The auction sale of the works left in his studio, held in the spring of 1880, furnished a still more surpassing expression of public regard.

The winter weather was violently inclement, yet a large public hall was filled with loving friends and anxious buyers from all the principal cities of the Union. Pictures that could have been purchased before his death for hundreds of dollars sold readily for as many thousands; and friends and strangers vied with each other for the slightest touch of the burning soul that was cold forever. The same enthusiasm that he had given so freely to the people in his life, was paid by them to his memory in the distribution of his works.

When Rimmer's exhibition took place, many thought that his drawings should become the property of the Museum; and an effort was made by those immediately connected with that institution to collect money for that purpose. Three hundred dollars were raised; the Museum, out of its scanty store, gave a like sum; and twelve of the artist's drawings were purchased, some of which are included among the illustrations of the present volume.

Personally, Hunt won friends by the irresistible charm of wit, knowledge of human nature, of picturesque, inspiring conversation, and of rare power of receiving and giving an impression. He could be personal if he chose, or unimpersonal if he would. Rimmer saw human nature, but could not govern it. His sense of self-protection was too severe for general popularity.

It is to be noted that the Japanese educators who were in Boston during the exhibition of Dr. Rimmer's works spent more time in examining them than in viewing any thing else in the building.

When the Rimmer exhibition opened, the public seemed scarcely to have heard of the dead artist. He was supposed to be an American; but, if so, it was evident that he must be accepted as an anticipator of ordinary art-growth by at least a hundred years, for there were in the works exhibited, compositions, ideas, and possibilities not to be looked for in the first century and a half of any country's art. The first public notice of the exhibition was the following letter, which appeared in " The Boston Daily Advertiser:" —

Allow me to call attention to an exhibition of the works of Dr. Rimmer, now open at the Museum of Fine Arts.

It comprises many of his paintings, as well as drawings, — indeed, specimens of all his various styles and kinds of work, — and affords a unique opportunity for the study of this powerful, if one-sided, genius.

Whatever reserves would have to be made in judging them as works of art, and admitting that the impression made by his off-hand blackboard-work was still stronger, yet the power of figure-drawing here shown is very remarkable, and should not be neglected by those interested in the matter.

                                                                J. E. C.

46. EVENING

# CHAPTER XVII.

### OBSERVATIONS ON ART AND LIFE.

HE following extracts from the writings of Dr. Rimmer are made with a view to showing, both his ideas concerning art, and the wide range over which his thought extended. Many of them are from the note-books of his pupils. Much suggests itself which might be remarked concerning them, did they not best speak for themselves.

———

Art can have no existence in any community in which the imaginative art is not recognized, or in which the foundation principles of an artistic education are not sufficiently axiomatic to give direction to an artist's aims in sound and discriminating criticism.

———

To describe mere forms, or imitate mere color, requires no other than mechanical skill, and gratifies no other than a visual want, the sense of form and the sense of color being among the commonest of human attributes; no people being so rude as not, at some time, to have given proof of the possession of these faculties.

———

Art is a science, so far as the use of its material is concerned, and so far as its methods and principles may be brought within measurable and cognizable limits. Thus, in color, the combining of two colors will produce a third. In perspective, the centre of the field of vision is the point of human sight. In human expression, an emotion may be described by the action of the features alone, or by the action of the limbs and body.

Every element of artistic power having its laws, the separation of them, one from another, for the purpose of discovery of these laws, becomes a matter of necessity in the effort to bring them within cognizable limits, as measurable facts. In this investigation, art, through the sources of its intelligence, is found to have, as a basis, the following elementary conditions: viz., form, proportion, size, motion, expression, composition, color, light and shade, perspective subject, etc.

Each of these, again, is found to have its laws, which are easily reduced to the limits of given formulas, as are phases of any other cognizable quality of a thing.

––––––––––

Special departments of art, or specialities in art, embrace but a portion of the elements of art.

––––––––––

The principles of art have no necessary connection with the technical methods of artists, more than the principles of harmony or instrumentation in the science of music have a necessary connection with the style of the composer; but as the style of the composer and the method of the artist are alike favorable or unfavorable to certain themes, these — having no place in any other place, in any other department, and being altogether matters of taste — must not be taken into account in any work as a part of the theme itself.

––––––––––

An artist's theme may be any thing, from the most important event in history down to the merest copy of nature in a landscape or other visual object.

––––––––––

The highest exercise of intelligence in art consists in the embodiment of the greatest number of elementary principles.

––––––––––

As perfection in any thing purely imaginative must be a sentimental abstraction, every work of art arising from this source must be a work of feeling and emotion, consequently a representative of the artist's ideal: by this it is discovered that the principles of art are only the means to an end; and, consequently, that in a school of art the elementary basis should constitute one branch of study, and matters of taste and imagination another branch.

One must be susceptible to impressions, and capable of reproducing them, but never be carried away by enthusiasm.

---

Above all things, proportion should be cultivated. When drawing the head, you must think of the feet. Look out for whole quantities. See things accurately as a whole, and details will take care of themselves. You are just as capable of judging as any one.

---

Depend on your own judgment; act independently. Persist in effort and self-reliance. Be more determined, and not depend on the opinion of others.

---

After the artistic anatomy, you should have exercise, and compose what is fine in the foot, hand, etc.

---

Make your men deep-chested and narrow-waisted, like a lion; for we live in this world not by let, but by opposition.

No figure can be fine in which the joints are not fine.

The knee is the finest joint in the body, and every detail of its mechanism and proportions should be carefully studied.

The thigh is the noblest part of the body. Avoid skeleton outlines; make no display of technical anatomy.

---

A work of art should be something more than the solution of a problem in science.

---

In the female head, passions are intensified by a display of the sensibilitie' in the male head, the passions are intensified by a display of the physical energ'

---

Anatomical elements are the same in all men: points of interest diffe' stations differ.

52.   BATTLE OF THE AMAZONS

COURTESY, FOGG ART MUSEUM, HARVARD UNIVERSITY; LOUISE E. BETTENS FUND.

53.   TO THE CHARGE

Always arrange your lights and shadows before commencing your picture. Have one high light, the other lights subordinate to that, and have the high light near the centre of your picture. It is a good plan to have a small part (not too much) left indefinite, mysterious, — left to the imagination.

---

Never use black very much. In white flowers, use brown and yellow, rather than black, with your white. In sketching trees, show the roots, if you can, in some places. Don't use much cadmium, and that with care.

---

In order to become true artists in figures, we must have knowledge of character. A young female head is something like a child's.

---

In sketching upon the beach, endeavor to introduce sand-hills.

---

In sketching from nature, begin with a tree, or something in the foreground, then draw the horizon, then the intervening distance.

Have your grass run in one general direction. In rocks, notice if they are stratified or bowlders. Birds which have large bills have large feet.

If persons have a certain number of fingers, they are likely to have the same number of toes.

In pictures, be careful to keep the shadows broad and unbroken.

In designing figures, it is best to have them looking in a somewhat different direction from that in which they are advancing.

Dead branches on a tree are usually on the north side.

---

When you see pictures, think what is the plan of a picture.

Have high light lighter than background, and shadow darker than background. This is the highest form of representation.

The dark side of a picture can have a lighter background.

Rembrandt, Rubens, Van Dyke, and Allston made shadows darker than background.

————————

There is something in color apart from form. I believe in color for the sake of color. I believe in adjusting your color with perfect exactness, painting with due regard to drapery, etc. In short, make a picture worthy the name of picture: these unalterable and alterable quantities show what goes to determine form of action. Let every piece of drapery go somewhere: don't make ambiguous folds. Show where it begins, and where it ends.

————————

Commence foreshortened figures with the part nearest to you. In making drapery, do not obscure the masculine proportions. What is true first, then what is fine. The size of the feet determine the size of the head: very small heads have large bodies, and *vice versa*.

————————

Nothing can be more beautiful than the way in which the arm is connected with the chest in the *Venus de Milo*.

*Atlas* is the most preposterous of all statues. The best study of the profile view of a female figure is the *Venus de Medici;* the best front view, the *Venus de Milo*.

————————

Expression is every thing. A German's head has more intelligence, kindness, good-humor, and seriousness, than any other: still it has its peculiar type.

————————

The *Venus de Medici* has a small head, the object being art, and not what is fine. These things must be settled, — this matter of proportion: a hair's breadth in the size of the head will necessitate a change in the body.

————————

Art is not a scholarly matter, but one of feeling and sensibility: your sense of action and proportion should be active.

————————

Make original drawings, especially those who are studying earnestly.

Never make a line that does not mean something. Full chest, flat back, high shoulders, short neck, large facial and small cerebral section, are characteristics of low types of man.

---

Draw according to feeling. Feel how a woman or a man looks; think less of quantities: unless you mean to have a model pose for you always, you must in some way learn these principles of the construction of the body; by studying anatomy, you will learn them in a measure. If you work from a model, you will give the peculiarities which that person has, instead of the ideal that you should give. If you have learned these principles, you can draw figures in any position. Notice how a bird looks when it is alighting, and draw that.

---

The human family is divided into three kinds, — a maxillary head, a nasal, and a vertical. See in a head its degree of development, and how far from, or near, the animal head. Every head must have something of the animal in quality or quantity; the more perfectly developed the brain, the more advanced and perfect the foot and hand, or leg or arm.

---

You can determine the scale of an animal by seeing how far the leg protrudes.

---

When a thing is fine to you, it is a representation of your own feeling, and it is fine.

---

Act liberally. Don't be influenced by schools. In the fine old pictures, there is no system: the men had much feeling, and were in a position where they could cultivate it. Cultivate your feeling.

---

Draw men, not women: you will weaken your artistic power if you do otherwise. From eight to eight and one-half heads in the Apollo. Women's heads are larger than men's. The best artists have disregarded this, and made the proportions like man.

One must be susceptible to impressions, and capable of reproducing them, but never be carried away by enthusiasm.

———

Above all things, proportion should be cultivated. When drawing the head, you must think of the feet. Look out for whole quantities. See things accurately as a whole, and details will take care of themselves. You are just as capable of judging as any one.

———

Depend on your own judgment; act independently. Persist in effort and self-reliance. Be more determined, and not depend on the opinion of others.

———

After the artistic anatomy, you should have exercise, and compose what is fine in the foot, hand, etc.

———

Make your men deep-chested and narrow-waisted, like a lion; for we live in this world not by let, but by opposition.

No figure can be fine in which the joints are not fine.

The knee is the finest joint in the body, and every detail of its mechanism and proportions should be carefully studied.

The thigh is the noblest part of the body. Avoid skeleton outlines; make no display of technical anatomy.

———

A work of art should be something more than the solution of a problem in science.

———

In the female head, passions are intensified by a display of the sensibilities: in the male head, the passions are intensified by a display of the physical energies.

———

Anatomical elements are the same in all men: points of interest differ as the stations differ.

47. FIGHTING LIONS

A statue of fine proportions is finer in proportion as the bulk is greater, within certain visual limits. When a statue is to be of great size, something of the proportions of men of the finest development should be given to it, that its size, which is an element of proportion, affecting the sensibilities, may not be contradicted by the personalities of its individual forms.

---

The vices and virtues of personal character stand in closest relation to the vices and virtues of personal ornamenture.

---

No intelligent idea of the human head can be had without a knowledge of the planes of the face.

---

The human proportions are the vertical proportions. The animal proportions are the horizontal proportions.

---

Nothing can exceed the beauty of the natural outline of a well-formed head. It should never be altogether obscured, nor its natural proportions defaced.

---

The hair and beard relate to the physical constitution (suppositional). The eye relates to the intellect. The mouth relates to the animal passions and the appetites.

---

The jaws of women are seldom strong or strongly marked.

---

Men gesticulate less than women.

---

The ear is an element of proportion only. When the ears are coarse, the hands and feet are coarse, and *vice versa.*

---

The beard may hide the features, but can never dominate in the expression of an intellectual head.

The forehead above the eyebrow is an element of proportion only.

---

Never exaggerate or overdo in any thing. A kindly expression will beautify the coarsest features. A good expression in a good face, and a bad expression in a bad face, represent the widest extremes of character.

---

Neither the ghastly nor the bloody should ever be represented.

---

The prevailing expression of countenance denotes the prevailing temper of the mind.

---

The descent towards the animal form in the human head is towards the animal in human nature, and not towards the animal as it exists in animal nature.

Details of the face become more manlike as the outline approaches the vertical.

It should be noticed in reference to its artistic uses, that the size of the head relates rather to the perfection and activity of the whole physical economy than to the intellect.

The size of the brain has no special connection with the strength of the understanding, other than as described above. The cerebral part of the head is an element of proportion only, and, without the facial part, is meaningless.

Any covering may hide the head above the brow without greatly changing the expression of the face. When the forehead is covered, the planes of the face determine the character.

Mixed forms describe mixed peculiarities of character.

Individual characteristics are represented in all races by the same peculiarities of form; there being but one type of structure for all mankind.

Surroundings attach themselves to persons; and modes of life, to types of head. The highest type, the best to represent highest conduct.

---

Do not allow yourself to caricature.

No attempt should be made to draw or model by the use of any unit or standard of proportions: if the sensibilities are not sufficient for the work, the workman is no artist.

No standard of proportions can supplant the feeling in the production of any work of art. A fine work will vivify, but never should enslave, the artist, whether sculptor, poet, or musician.

-----

To copy a fine statue or picture, no more makes, or helps to make, one a fine sculptor or painter than copying a fine poem makes one a fine poet.

-----

The things which are fine in music, poetry, or sculpture, may be copied, but they can never be invented except by an original effort of the soul.

-----

Every work of art is the result of a new discovery of one's own powers, and an exact measure of the capabilities or limitations.

-----

Science is to art what brick-making is to architecture.

-----

Order and repose are the soul of the works of Greek art.

-----

Mere portrait-sculpture belongs to the mechanical arts.

-----

Portrait-painting is susceptible of the highest artistic excellence.

-----

Remember! That the faculty of reason is below the faculty of worship; and the Protestants may, in striving to admit the mind to the path of duty by the one, draw the soul's attention from the holiest promptings of the other, which the Catholics so much do honor, as the safer master for the conscience.

We are more exact in great, all-important things, if we are truly great, than we are in small things.  There are some who have a genius for minutiæ, small things being best covered by their understanding; and there is a natural field for their microscopic powers, which, in our efforts to be perfect, we cannot do without.

---

(*Written on a lady's card.*)   Only think — Socrates might catch a gape from a fool, or a beggar move a king to yawn: think of it!

---

Pity him that has neither genius, talent, money, nor good looks.

---

Hearts need homes, as well as heads.

---

Individuality is above all.

---

An artist must hold himself aloof from the subject of art, or he will be weakened by its influence.   Unless he does this, he cannot judge himself or others.

---

When did any thing ever receive the approval of all the thousand different tempers in the world?

---

I have no reason for wishing to remain as a teacher of drawing.   My object is to be at the head of a school of art.

---

Some men, in their natures, represent the soul of things; and some, the body of things.   The one is for the things that are for the good of all; the other, for the good of self against all others.   The latter, from the nature of their endowment, reap what the others sow; exist under the reign of law and order that the others preserve.   The one class are the patient, the working, constant poor; the other are the scheming, the inconstant, rich.

As long as the world stands, some men will be better situated than others; but why should one man ever tremble before another? Did not our Lord Jesus cry out against the oppressor, and die for the poor? Why should one man have more of the good of this world, save as he merits it in all righteousness, than another?

---

Consume the vicious with fire and sword; cut off the oppressor from the face of the earth; destroy the consumer of other men's labor. Why should sin triumph before our eyes? Why should the vanities of the rich pollute the eyes of our children? Before God, what right has any man to any thing that impoverishes another? Who shall dare say that one man is not as much in need of happiness as another?

---

Through the mind's sensitiveness to impressions, and its ability to reason upon them, it acquires a knowledge of the things which act upon it. And hence, by the processes in an intellectual form, in the things that correspond to it, the world is reflected in it; and in turn, from the inner world, or world of intelligence, by the transmuting power of thought and emotion, is reflected into the external world, in works of art, poetry, and music, in shapes that bear at once the impressions of our feelings, the likeness of the things which excite them to activity.

---

Much of what we think belongs to the external world, belongs to ourselves: it being the case, that while we think we are looking at the things about us, and contemplating their excellences, we are in reality looking into our own soul, moving in its boundless space and worlds upon worlds, contemplating its endless and immeasurable beauties. And hence things purely intellectual have an intellectual origin: music, painting, sculpture, architecture, poetry, and all that ministers to them by processes of thought or feeling, belong to the spirit.

For though the material world (in the forces that underlie and sustain the things composing it) has a life of its own, — always right and in the right, — yet, in these things which I have just mentioned, it is as void of being as though it were space itself.

Seeing, hearing, and feeling are called into activity by the things that are about us; but the activity to perceive and to do, which underlies these acts, enabling us to perform them (as well as the emotions that accompany them), and the remembrance of them, and their association with one another, all belong to ourselves.

Trees, rocks, mountains, and valleys are beautiful, only because there is in us a world of beauty, to which such things correspond. If it were not for that, what would they be to us? What could they be?

Thus, when we look at an object to discover its qualities, we but place ourselves in communication with it by processes of sight or other senses (for all mean cognizance), to see what judgment our nature, out of the depth of our being, will render to us concerning it; and that which it sends up to us, that which it creates for us, that,—in the nature of the activities that give it being,—*that* is ours!

———————

Form, in the arts of sculpture and painting, is wholly visual; as these arts themselves are for the gratification of the imagination in its visual elements and desires (relating to being through the possibilities of sight) in matters of sentiment and intelligence.

Every sense has a sphere of its own, in which the soul may exercise its faculties; and that of sight is first, because it embraces the largest number and the greatest variety of conditions. Form accompanies being, and describes it.

Every finite quantity has a limit. The terminal limit of a quantity is its outline. An outline describes not only the thing having it, but also the space that the thing having it occupies, and hence describes the space.

When there is no closure, there is no outline. Mere open lines of any form describe nothing but themselves, or parts of things which belong to some form of closure. The closest line, in its simplest form, is a circle.

The open line is any line within which there is nothing enclosed. The straight line is the best example of lines of this class.

Although the same outline encloses both matter and space, we think only of matter and its immediate secondary relations,—its locality, etc. This, though never first in the abstract, never escapes us; while we seldom think of mere room in connection with being.

Form is the accompaniment of being, as quantity and extent are the accompanying conditions of vital existence.

To the visual sense, or the cognizing power that lies behind the operations of

49.   FALLING FIGURES

48.   THE POOR MAN HAS NOTHING TO LOSE

sight, form is an expression of existence; and, from the connection usually subsisting between form and quality, the kind of form is taken as proof of the kind of quality.

The connection subsisting between form and quality in every thing relating to orders and classes is complete.

The form of one lion stands for the forms and qualities of all lions; that of one horse, for all horses; and if the forms of different animals be so placed, or are so found, that they may be seen together, they not only represent the different qualities found in each, but stand, besides, for the difference between them.

What is true in this respect of classes is equally true of individual beings; with the difference, that classes, and even family characteristics, are easily discovered, because, being common to so many, the common form includes them; while individual characteristics, being the result of that modification of general qualities that comes from the activities of special mental and physical conditions, must first be discovered in their individual significance before they can be associated with the being's accompanying form.

As class peculiarities must also be individual peculiarities to the extent that individuals have a common form or character, the portrait or statue of an animal must stand for all that the animal itself would stand for visually.

Form, in this respect, embraces all the external manifestations of life.

Being does not depend upon form, nor does a being think of his form for existence or action. Yet as organized beings have determinate forms, and these forms have not only general and individual characteristics, but also sentimental and secondary relations that keep them outside of themselves, as it were, fixed in that degree and state of their being, and as one or the other of these must constitute the motive for imitating their peculiarities, the following classification may serve to keep that motive in view: —

*First.* The mere portrait or likeness of a man or animal, — mere latent form; or, form with only such evidence of life and activity as is necessary to exhibit class or individual traits of physical character.

In the first and simplest degree, form is within the reach of the ordinary mechanical power of observation, or the mechanical use of the power of observation, — proportion and comparison. Within the scope of this, the first quality of things, every man is an artist, for every man possesses the power of observation and comparison sufficiently strong to enable him to describe the difference in the form of things; and any thing that can be made out by observation and comparison can be imitated by observation and comparison, if sufficient time is given and pains taken with the work. Some possess the faculty of comparison to so perfect a degree as to enable them to do in an hour what others could scarcely do in a day; yet, in kind, the faculty is the same in all, and is possessed by some in the highest excellence who are quite destitute of every other power of art. To make a literal copy requires, for the time being, the subjection of every faculty but comparison, and, if followed long for itself, destroys the higher love for art in worth of imagination and the ideal.

Mere latent form in the simplest expression of external being, without emotion or action, if selected,—and one may select, whose power as an artist enables him to discover in what the actual furnishes the thought of the ideal,—often rivals the ideal in comparison that may be made of mere physical excellence, in its highest development, with the physical excellence that subdued and shaped it to the requirements of the highest beauty; becomes the ideal,—the natural compared with the beautiful. Such would be the actual in its best manifestations; while, in this department, to discriminate is to rise above it.

Mere latent form, whether in its degree or in the power required to produce it, takes all things alike, and as they are,—mineral, vegetable, and animal; producing faithfully from some original, and believing in what is before it. Most of the sculpture and painting of the present day lies within this sphere, the different degrees of merit in different works being but different degrees of mere naturalness.

It must be repeated, that too close attention to mere common form for the purpose of becoming acquainted with its nature and manifestations tends to weaken the higher perceptions of sentimental and imaginative excellence, and, consequently, to destroy in the mind the distinction between the mere natural and its variations, and the higher type, or sentimental, and its varieties.

Naturalism in form has its use, for it is the description; but while, on the one hand, it reaches the ideal, as, on the other, it descends to the grotesque and vile, by itself it is the lowest of all the departments of art, and requires the least amount of talent for its exercise.

Naturalism, as an element, will be more fully considered in its place.

*Second.* Form in action, or form made to represent action; the action or story being of the first importance, the form being but the means by which the action is made apparent,—rage, hate, mirth, melancholy, love, despair, etc., as primary motives.

51.  THE SOWER

50.  FEEDING HER BIRDS

This degree is still descriptive; for, though higher in motive and wider in scope than the former, it is yet limited to present conduct and condition, leading the mind more to what the thing is doing, and to its condition, than to the thing itself.

The chief interest being dramatic, historic, or scenic, in which last may be included the effect of all that relates to the action or massing and grouping of multitudes, architectural groupings, interior ornamentation, the effect of different kinds of material, etc.

Though the scenic is of necessity included, because in painting it is often, and always may be, employed to heighten the effect of some central personal passion, it cannot of itself constitute the central motive, where form, as it relates to passion, is considered.

The more special passional activity is made to appear, the more personal it must be. The more closely it is defined, that is, the more limited its scope, its possibilities, and its suggestions, the more circumscribed must be its theme, the narrower the sympathies that surround it, and the less enduring the pleasure that flows from it.

The more positive or violent an action or passion is made to appear, the lower are the faculties that must examine it, and the fewer the persons that will sympathize with it; since individual modes of thought or conceptions of character, when given in a form that leaves nothing to the imagination, are seldom found to correspond to the types of similar things existing in the mind of the beholder.

The show of wounds and blood, actual shooting and stabbing no one of sensibility can indulge in: nor should special pains be taken to exhibit them in any way, or by any means; because, from their very nature, such things excite emotions of their own, independent of the place, or the use that may be made of them. The splitting of skulls and the spattering of brains are natural horrors, that, painted by any one, beget only feelings of contempt for the sensibilities of the artist that could perpetrate such an outrage.

Clawed demons, bat-wings with hooks, scaly dragons with forked tails, scorpions, centipedes, serpents, witches with hooked nails or beast-like canine teeth, cloven feet, and all such things, are as vicious in art as in poetry. Only those who feel themselves unequal to the task of exhibiting the intellectual or moral condition of things or circumstances will resort to mere physical characteristics, or use of external signs or implements. To frighten, terrify, or disgust by the use of horrible forms, when that to which they refer is of and within the sphere of intelligence, is to appeal to the sense when we should appeal to reason, to fear rather than to judgment. Just where an artist's power fails, just where he cannot comprehend or command his subject, just there the wavering, the compound of his intellect, must be evident in his works.

The canvas and clay can take no other form than those the artist can give it. The subject chosen is but the opportunity to do, the occasion where his thoughts may be expressed, a sphere in which he may create things after his own choice in the order of the impulse that moves him. If his perception of things is weak or exceptional, his works will be weak and exceptional. If he is ignorant, if he is in love with mere prettiness or fashion or display, his men and women will be the fitting representatives of his emotion. If he thinks nobly, having manly perceptions of men, conceives right and wrong justly, and receives impressions of things without prejudice, each can but be apparent in his work, making in superior action superior men and things. The errors of ignorance, as an artist gets on, will always be known from the errors of sensibility.

When an action has the character of all actions of the kind, an expression the character of all expressions of the kind, and the interest is of so wide a scope that all kindred interests may be included, the work ceases to be personal and individual; for it lies within the limit of the ideal, where action, form, and condition are typical, generic, and unimmediate, resulting from the widest sympathy in the artist, who by it extends his emotion over the broadest area of men.

For it is not just the thing seen in stone or on the canvas, that makes the work a work of art, but all the conceptions of life and circumstance that the soul has cognizance of, that may be suggested by the stone or canvas.

How, in the sphere of that which is represented, either in emotion or condition, can one whose every energy is spent in mastering the form of a thing, ever reach its spirit? and, without the spirit or intellectual relation of things in art, what must be the purpose or the ideal?

In giving great prominence to action and emotion, in whatever particular, we approach the sensational, the sphere of actual events, where art is unknown.

That which is done for us, we do not do for ourselves. If the chief interest in a picture is the national flag, the painter cannot be entitled to any applause we may give the picture for its sake: he has taken advantage of our affections, rather.

If he makes an empty cradle, and places a rattle and a pair of little shoes beside it with a mother weeping over them, he is entitled to no credit for the sympathy he may have awakened: in such, rather, he has wounded us, in exposing the wounds of others. And yet such incidents, in the hand of those who can use them wisely in one form or another, lie at the foundation of every thing that is fine in painting and in sculpture.

———————

Neither justice, order, nor truth is absolute, only as it is discovered by the unfolding of nature and intelligence.

———————

There are certain laws, as regards the distinguishing traits or features of different types and nationalities, — of lower and higher order of intelligence, of lower and higher order of animal life even.

———————

I believe that the hope and future of the country depends upon the poor people, the humble classes, and not upon the rich and aristocrats. All the virtues, braveries, and sacrifices are exemplified in the poor: they have written the sublimest pages of history.

# CHAPTER XVIII.

### RECOLLECTIONS AND ANECDOTES.

R. RIMMER'S pupils tell many incidents, which perhaps more clearly indicate the true character of the man than could pages of discussion. Speaking of the late William M. Hunt, he once said, "Mr. Hunt is a good deal larger man than he is a painter, and he is a pretty large painter."

The daughter of Professor A., an eminent scientist, remarked to Dr. Rimmer that her father did not agree with his theory upon a certain subject. "So much the worse for your father," was the uncompromising answer.

He once said that the most difficult thing which he was ever asked to do was to draw a hand pointing directly towards the observer, and added that he had to think a moment before doing it.

When one of his daughters suggested the propriety of his publishing a volume of his remarks in art, — something similar to Hunt's "Art Talks," — he objected that " he could not respect such a thing, he did not believe in it, and thought it beneath his dignity as an artist."

He was once asked, during a lecture, to draw on the board, for the benefit of his class, what he considered the ideal human face. He replied that this was something he could not do to his own satisfaction. "And, should I attempt it," he added, turning with a smile to the one making the request, "I fear it would be so ugly-looking a fellow that you would not accept it."

When drawing upon the blackboard, the doctor would often carry on a most interesting conversation concerning art or other matters. This displeased some of his hearers, and gave rise to the objection occasionally raised against him that he did not confine himself to his subject. When the artists of the National Academy asked him to deal only with art anatomy, leaving his theories of art for some other occasion, he replied, "But I don't want to spend all my time teaching: I want to have some pleasure in speaking of art."

Speaking of Massachusetts people, he once said, "When you find a good one, he is real good all through. You can no more get around him in knowledge than you can get over him in wisdom, or under him in integrity. You cannot go to windward of him in caution, or in Greek and Latin."

Of Salmon, the English marine artist who visited this country fifty years ago, and some of whose pictures are in the Charlestown Navy Yard Museum, Dr. Rimmer said, "He was a fine painter. One seldom sees better marines."

Once when painting a Madonna, he said, in answer to the remark of a friend, "Instead of making a glory around the head, I wish to make the whole body a glory."

It is related that on the first day of one of his classes in Studio Building, there came for admission a lady and her child, belonging to one of the most esteemed families of Boston. Not having a ticket, she was refused admission by the attendant at the door. "But I am Mrs. ——," she said: "we are friends of Dr. Rimmer." — "Dr. Rimmer gave me imperative orders," answered the attendant, "to admit no one without a ticket." The lady went away astonished and offended. A friend, learning the incident, spoke to Dr. Rimmer of the matter. "I have given my orders, and they must be exactly obeyed," was the only reply that Dr. Rimmer would give.

He once sketched on the blackboard some horses drawing a load. On examining the efforts of his class in their sketch-books, he said with much warmth, "But why don't you make your horses draw?" Then, going quickly to the board, he wiped out the drawing, and made another, with the horses' heads bent to the earth, and every muscle straining, as if he would force his scholars to see the movement.

To Mr. F. P. Vinton, Dr. Rimmer observed, with reference to the former's portrait of Mr. Thomas Appleton: "It is a fine work, and it pleases me very much. It is the strongest work I have seen in Boston." And with a kindly smile he continued, "If I were to criticise it, I should say that it is, perhaps, almost too strong. You will do finer things, I have no doubt; but try to keep always something of the quality that you have in this portrait."

One of the doctor's pupils visited him while he was painting upon a hilly landscape, and, noticing the peculiar direction or inclining of the trees on the hillside, asked, "Do trees always grow at right angles with a hill?" The doctor half-unconsciously replied, "I don't know. Don't they?" as though his mind was occupied with matter beyond the present work or the person addressing him.

Dr. Rimmer admired the human figure to an extravagant degree, but always kept it at arm's-length; and he was absolutely unable to recognize the fact that an entirely nude male model was a necessity, and could be studied with propriety by females. Some of his more serious pupils did not coincide with him in this view. The doctor's delicacy was extreme in this matter, and he would never consent to be present or to give instruction at times when they insisted upon such advantages.

The wounded dignity and mental pain that Dr. Rimmer endured may be easily imagined, on being told by a gentleman, whose daughter was a pupil of the doctor's, that he was informed that a male model was allowed to go about the schoolroom without clothing. "My daughter," added the gentleman, "is anxious to study with you; but, if this nude model promenading is permitted, I cannot consent to it." The doctor retorted that he had a family of daughters of his own, and believed he was not wanting in a sense of propriety.

His class went sometimes, in the old and early days, to the gloomy galleries of the Boston Athenæum, where the lower hall, now reading-room, was crowded with the dusty collection of casts and marbles. There his admiration for the antique, when the antique was good, was strongly shown; and, at the same time, his lofty independence of all masters, and his poetical appreciation of purity in art, was made very clear. It was on one of these delightful occasions that he said, pointing to the cast of Michael Angelo's *Morning*, "That is the Black Sea: this" — the *Torso Belvidere*, about which he was explaining — "is the ocean."

"One morning in class, in 1865," writes a pupil, "the doctor was walking up and down the aisle, while we were copying his sketch on the board. When he passed me I handed him a volume of Gilchrist's Life of Blake, which I had just brought from the Athenæum. He took a few turns more up and down, intent upon the illustrations with his eyes, which could see more in a minute than most could in days, and laying the book by me said, in a low and solemn voice, 'Mr. S., that man had more genius than Michael Angelo.' Then, erasing his drawing, in a few moments there was another; and I fancied that a ray from William Blake had touched him."

"As three of our little girls," relates another, "had shown some aptness in drawing, we were anxious that they should receive the best training, and consequently we applied to Dr. Rimmer. 'Bring me their drawings,' said the busy teacher, 'and I will tell you if it is worth your while to spend as much money as I must ask you.' We took their childish efforts to him. He quickly turned over the drawings, giving no heed to well-drawn lines or good shading — for the children had had some careful training — until he came to a picture which evidently had received no teacher's direction. It was a purely childish fancy, — a scene in fairy-land, — and so crude in its execution, that I had hesitated about numbering it with the other drawings. I shall never forget the eagerness with which he caught up the picture, nor the expression which came into his eyes as he said, 'There! That means something! The child had something to say! I care nothing for your perfect copies. There is no real art in mere designs. Many call a man an artist if he can take a good portrait. If this is all he can do, he is no artist. What the age needs is more of the ideal. The imagination must be brought out and cultured. If your children come to me, I shall take them to the blackboard, and try to find out what they love to draw, no matter what it is, and encourage them in that direction. I shall endeavor to lead them into a true knowledge of form.' "

"Don't go into the galleries to copy," Dr. Rimmer said to one of his pupils who was going to Europe. "Study the pictures there, making pencil memoranda if you like; but do your copying away from the galleries. Otherwise, you will settle down to doing nothing else. In copying, and even in drawing from life, you are only learning the alphabet of art. It is time that you began to express yourself. Keep your eyes open to impressions, wherever you are, and do the best you can to record your impressions."

One of the artist's most appreciative admirers relates the following anecdote: " A poor boy who had, I thought, some talent, and whose parents were too poor to pay his tuition, wanted to attend Dr. Rimmer's classes. I spoke to the latter about it. 'Send him, of course,' said he: 'I ask no pay from the poor.' The boy began his studies, and I thought no more about the matter until I received from Dr. Rimmer a bill for the boy's tuition amounting to thirty dollars. Somewhat surprised, I asked at the first opportunity why he charged any thing at all, and why the bill was sent to me. 'I am informed that the boy's father is abundantly able to pay, sir. I wish to have no talk about the matter. I hold you responsible, sir.' With these words, uttered in an excited manner, and accompanied by a most imperious wave of the hand, he left me. This was my first personal experience with that side of Dr. Rimmer's character, and it was the last I desired. I afterward met him several times, but he seemed always under a little restraint. His action was thoughtless and unreasonable, but my regard for his genius continued unaltered."

On one occasion, when the doctor was delivering some lectures before a school whose master was presumptuous and self-asserting, a question of anatomy came up, wherein the latter took issue with the doctor, and walked up to the blackboard to explain his superiority. "All right," said the doctor. "You take one board, and I will take the other, and we will see who best understands this subject." The man of words took his seat, and the artist continued his drawing.

He had an appreciation of humor when not allied to coarseness, and was always interested in the political and social cartoons and paragraphic journalism of the day. A friend tells of one evening when the conversation was upon Greek mythology. Something gave it a humorous turn, and the doctor took his pencil, and made some burlesque sketches of mythological and historical characters and incidents; such, for instance, as a very questionable Leander swimming across an unpoetical Hellespont, while a realistic Hero signalled him to safety with the light of a kerosene-oil lamp.

When drawing upon the blackboard, Dr. Rimmer indulged in a habit of whistling in a low tone as a distraction from pain of body or mind. A little girl, who attended the class one day with her mother, noticed this, and, when she came home, began to draw, at times stopping to rest and whistle. Her mother, overhearing this variation, asked what she was doing, and received the reply, "Why, I'm whistling, so that I can draw. Dr. Rimmer whistles when he draws."

He went with a friend one day to a New-York art-store to see a half-life-size picture of a male figure. He looked at it for about two minutes, and said to his companion, "Come away, B.: the position of the figure is an impossibility, the color is bad, and the lips are sensuous."

Dr. Rimmer once attended a party where there was a celebrated performer on the flute, who entertained the company with the music of that instrument. The doctor, who played well, was also asked to contribute, but declined, saying, "One lion for a party is enough."

Dr. Rimmer studied people with apparently unconcerned persistency, taking advantage of every opportunity which presented itself. When he went to New York, he preferred the boat to the cars, always securing a state-room in advance. After arriving

52.   BATTLE OF THE AMAZONS

53.   TO THE CHARGE

on board, he would walk about among the passengers in search of some interesting character, and, when he found one, would invite him to share his room. In this way the doctor made some very amusing and valuable acquaintances.

Dr. Rimmer disliked "a white cravat, gold-bowed spectacles, and white felt or beaver hat," and was suspicious of men who wore them. Rings, chains, bracelets, and other jewelry ornaments were distasteful to him. He interpreted the wearing of these articles as showing "an earthly quality in the wearer." Of certain persons of pretence who thought that the world existed especially for their pleasure he said, "Heaven will, if we do not, change eventually in some way our democratic ferocity of self-conceit and dollar-greatness into a true aristocracy that will humble these turkey-buzzards that now gobble and strut so abominably in our midst." Of a distinguished clergyman, he writes: "He is a sharp, quick, bright-looking man; but he has a very sharp nose for a man of his profession." Of a certain art connoisseur he says in his East-Milton diary: "He is an intelligent man of some taste, but, I should think, would be the terror of artists, regarded as an expert, a critic, in the perception of beauty and deformity. It is strange that the popular progress and success of an artist depend upon the favor of such men. Happily he said nothing against my statue. I wonder if I can trust him?" Of another art "authority:" "Pshaw! what a supercilious nose; what a half-boorish, sneaking mouth; what a detestable play of muscles of the face; what a mixture of good feature and rascality of expression! How he seemed at a loss whether to jump on my back, and demand admission to my studio, or fall at my feet, and lick the blacking off my shoes! He puckers his mouth like a frivolous woman, and can faint or whine at a moment's notice. He wins his way by sneers and jests at the earnest world. He said that my statue was 'remarkable,' 'wonderful;' could not 'understand how I did it;' would 'call in the ladies,' who appeared polite and well-bred. How can sensible women find in such languishing imbecility any thing to admire?"

A lady who is well known for her enthusiastic interest in art wished the sculptor to make a bust of her daughter who had lately died; but his work was not a success. Recording this event in his diary, he says, "Mrs. F. has just relieved me of my most troublesome labor, and paid me most generously for my efforts. The Mohammedans say that women have no souls: I say that they are all soul. If I had succeeded, the credit would have been due to Miss W."

Of an artist who enjoyed an authoritative and well-preserved position as a judge, a sort of arbitrator of the destines of others, the doctor writes: "The long-looked-for Mr. —— was brought down by Mr. Perkins day before yesterday." After dissecting him in a just and-correct manner, he adds, "But there is one thing that I like about him ; and that is, an honest outspoken yes-and-no-ism, and he looks one square in the face."

On seeing some photographs of Canova's works, Rimmer observes : "He made some fine statues ; but, if I may venture an opinion on the works of so great an artist, I should say that he strains a little for effect, and has too much mannerism to be altogether agreeable. His *Hercules* is brutal, with many fine points, but execrable in attitude, and most offensive in its lines. Every thing that makes art beautiful in its manifestations is in his work sacrificed to mere action."

In this same East-Milton diary he writes : " I know of no one whose judgment I would rather have than my wife. She can perceive to perfection the nicest points and shades of difference in my work. What can others' praise do for me, or what make me happier than I am when she commends ? "

# CHAPTER XIX.

### DESCRIPTION OF ILLUSTRATIONS.

THE illustrations in this book will give, in some degree, an idea of the character of Dr. Rimmer's genius. Those taken from drawings have been selected with reference to reproduction by the heliotype process. Other drawings made with a fine-pointed pencil, some of them with the aid of a magnifying-glass, of interesting composition and representative character, cannot be reproduced except by the burin of the engraver.

Our civil war suggested many symbolic compositions, three of which are included in the list of illustrations. The historical significance of the one dedicated to the Fifty-fourth Regiment Massachusetts Volunteers is, that it was the first regiment composed of colored men sent to the war by the North, though commanded by a white man, Col. R. G. Shaw. The original drawing in pencil was exhibited in Boston in 1863, and photographs of it were sold for the benefit of the regiment. It represents the monster of slavery crouching beneath the palmetto; while four armed warriors go forth, in splendid movement and salutation, to attack him. They bear on their shields the sacred emblems of hope, faith, liberty, and light.

SECESSIA AND COLUMBIA is another of the war-drawings, as is also the one dedicated to the Forty-fourth Regiment Massachusetts Volunteers. Both are drawn in pencil. The latter is about the size of the original, while the first is greatly reduced.

Of the many sketches made in clay, as inspired by the same motive, none are in existence. Some of them the doctor desired to preserve; but a certainty of destruction followed every one, so that it became a belief with him that it was impossible to preserve them. In reply to some sympathetic words from a member of his family concerning this state of affairs, he would say, " Well, it is all past. Make believe that it happened a hundred years ago. Let us go on with what we have to do."

The character of the clay sketches was more personal than that of the drawings, and some of them were pathetic in their rendering of the painful condition of the negro in the war for the Union. They showed that their author understood the profound significance of the conflict in its political as well as artistic aspect.

The TRI-MOUNTAIN is the first sketch of a monumental group which Rimmer designed for the three hills of Boston. He made several large sketches of it in clay; and also desired one of his pupils to execute a sketch, in the hope that it might attract public attention. No good fortune, either to the artist or the public, was in store for this or any other of the numberless designs of a similar nature which he was constantly making.

The CENTAUR was made in odd hours, in 1871, without the employment of a model.

The FIGHTING LIONS were also executed in chance moments. They are the property of the Boston Art Club.

The FALLING GLADIATOR is one of a series of figures which the sculptor intended as illustrations of a story of ancient times, partly written before the figure was modelled.

The DEAD HUNTER AND HIS DOG is copied from a lithograph made while Rimmer was working at that art.

The MIDNIGHT RIDE is the tracing of a fine pencil-drawing, made when the artist was fourteen years old, as one of the illustrations of a poem by that name, and alluded to earlier in this volume.

The SOOTHSAYER may be taken as a good example of the artist's work of this kind.

The CALL TO ARMS is one of the drawings from the " Art Anatomy."

CUPID RELATING HIS ADVENTURES TO VENUS is the first sketch of the large picture already spoken of.

The water-color sketch is the only one the doctor ever executed.

There are four illustrations of parts of a subject entitled, AND SATAN CAME ALSO. This subject Dr. Rimmer treated in various ways, as it was a favorite one with him. In some of his drawings of Satan, the extreme curvature of the figure aroused the curiosity of one of his pupils; and she asked him the reason of it. He replied: " This curvature increases the idea of strength, and gives a sinister effect. I have often thought of making a statue of Satan. He should have great beauty, very great arrogance, and throughout the whole figure should be felt a certain warp of bone, muscle, and expression: thus producing a subtleness in keeping with the character of Satan."

Of the great range of subjects treated with more or less consideration by Dr. Rimmer, none were more varied and beautiful than that of MORNING. Previous to his forty-fifth year he was influenced by religious subjects, and the contests and trials of his own and his father's life. After this time, when he had assumed the *rôle* of a public lecturer, and formed wider relations with society, he was not incited to production by men or events, to any extent. The heroic character and national and historic position of John Brown did not affect him, nor win his admiration. The personality of men, at any given time, did not, indeed, produce any decided art-impression upon him. Abstract ideas, the powers and principles which move to great action, to complete retirement, to lofty contemplation, he sought to embody in forms of mighty beings, of grand nature, of wide and distant landscape, seen from commanding eminences. He exulted in compositions in which the soul looks down upon the world, in which all power of beast, all influence of forest, stream, and plain, are subservient to the exalted superiority of man.

Two out of a large number of sketches of MORNING are given. One represents a female figure reclining upon a hill overlooking a vast landscape; the other, a winged youth joyously holding up a surprised infant. These sketches are among the most poetical of Dr. Rimmer's works. Some other representations of MORNING are more extensive and elaborate: one where, in endless column, numberless figures are soaring through the air in impetuous and splendid movement, with wings outstretched, and crowns of light in their hands; another represents the air full of graceful and beautiful male and female figures descending to the earth; in still another an innumerable host of cupids are flying through the sky, and blowing trumpets to awaken the sleeping world.

The great variety with which he treated the same subject suggests the impression that he was not individual, but rather the medium through which the ideal world took form on paper or canvas.

It is said that one-fourth of all the drawings made by Dr. Rimmer were figures falling through the air. The principal one selected, NINE DAYS THEY FELL, was the best one for reproduction, though not the most perfect example.

The EVENING, or FALL OF DAY, is the largest of the artist's drawings on paper which has been preserved. It is forty by fifty inches in size, and drawn in colored chalk. It was exhibited soon after it was completed, in Boston and New York, without producing any notable impression.

The VICTORY, though a hastily made pen-and-ink study, shows the style of the artist's vigor, his directness and understanding of action and purpose.

The FENCING LESSON and DEAD SOLDIER are fair specimens of his foreshortening. His power in the drawing of horses is seen in the HORSES OF THE CHARIOT OF THE SUN. On several occasions Dr. Rimmer was asked to do some illustrative work, but for one reason or another nothing was consummated; but in 1878, when the labor-troubles in Fall River, Mass., were occupying the attention of the public, there were some allusions in the newspapers to the effect that the laborer had nothing to lose in the contentions between labor and capital, while the capitalist staked every thing. This unjust reflection caused the doctor to make the illustration of THE POOR MAN HAS NOTHING TO LOSE, for "The Porcupine," an illustrated and humoristic weekly published in Boston.

EMPEROR, WARRIOR, AND POET, or ROMAN HISTORY, is a drawing of a subject of which the artist was very fond. Human dignity and power as illustrated by imperial representatives like poets, emperors, and warriors, were special subjects of his contemplation and admiration. It was in his blood. Their history as characters of the world formed a large part of his enjoyment, and one of his most serious studies.

The different orders of architecture had their analogies with human types, and Dr. Rimmer often drew heads and figures to illustrate the various stages of the development of both. No principle of art, human nature, or mechanics, but was recognized by him. Nothing seemed to escape his piercing observation.

Painting was an uninterrupted pleasure with Dr. Rimmer; and in none of his efforts is the want of a surrounding world of art so apparent as in his struggles with color, in which he gained no reputation; and his paintings would hardly attract serious general attention as such. In the most successful of them, there is a tendency towards yellows and browns, which has led many people to conjecture that their author must have been afflicted with defective color-vision; while in others, in which there appears to be a determined effort to get rid of this tendency, the combinations are unpleasantly cold and inharmonious. Yet the artist loved color, and it was one of his fondest hopes to spend his old age in the enjoyment of painting. "My dear, we will revel in paint one of these days," was an oft-repeated and longing expression addressed to his youngest daughter. The two pictures which are the most successful in this respect, and which warrant the belief that he had the natural capacities of a painter and colorist of strength and quality, are the VENUS AND ADONIS, and MADONNA AND

54. LION IN THE ARENA

55. LION AND SNAKE

Child. With them ought also to be mentioned The Sentinel. As compositions they are worthy of the artist. The color of the Venus is rich and powerful, the drawing and construction masterly in parts. The Madonna is fine and tender; and the Sentinel, in its conception, statuesque.

As compositions Dr. Rimmer's pictures are more extensive and complete than his drawings. In them he seemed to go to the end of the expression of force, weight, and concentration. Some of them have a grand swing of arrangement; others, the most delicate touch of sentiment.

In a small picture of a shipwreck, where an enormous vessel is represented with her bow towards the spectator, the waves are made terribly and irresistibly destructive, not as a turbulent force of water as seen in mid-ocean in a great storm, when they break with the abruptness of a mountain ledge, overwhelming and crushing, but as a writhing, winding, serpent-like mass, which encloses and ingulfs without spray or tumult. You feel that a continent could not withstand this movement. Water becomes a fiend. The color of the picture is an unpleasant combination of green, blue, and black.

Nearly all of his paintings are too dark for any reproduction, except by the skill of the etcher or engraver. The Lion in the Arena, Lion and Snake, Flight and Pursuit, To the Charge, and The Battle of the Amazons were the best for illustration.

The foreground and middle distance in The Battle of the Amazons have many interesting groups and single figures that are lost in the reproduction. To a considerable degree the same may be said of To the Charge. The saddle of the flying Amazon is decorated with the heads of her enemies.

In no subject that he treated was there such full display of his genius for handling compositions containing many figures, motives, and masses, as in battle scenes,—often redundant in matter, but never lacking in comprehension.

Flight and Pursuit, or, as it was called in the pencil sketch, Oh for the Horns of the Altar! is the property of Mrs. C. H. Nichols of Providence, R.I. The Lion in the Arena belongs to Mrs. S. D. Warren of Boston.

The Master Builder is one of the artist's strange subjects, and has many interpretations, none of which are known to be the right one. Some say that it is based upon an Irish legend; others, that it illustrates human vanity in the figure and position of the Builder, and envy, as illustrated by the creeping curs and male figure. This picture is the property of Miss Minns of Boston.

The predominating elements of Rimmer's landscapes were vast plains, high mountains, imposing temples, regally arranged horses and riders, all displaying a love for knightly life. The illustration entitled FIGURES is from a sepia drawing. The left-hand figure is a very characteristic one.

Not the least of the peculiar traits that characterized Dr. Rimmer was a habit of tearing up a sketch, or knocking to pieces a clay model, as soon as it was done, or at the severe criticism of a friend. His practice of making drawings similar to the illustrations, and of models in clay for figures, groups, and monumental projects, was continuous; and these would, if counted, amount to thousands.

He delighted in constructing figures based upon some leading human trait, — many prominent men of the time were thus treated, — and he understood how to perfect a type of man that had deteriorated for one reason or another. It is one of the highest elements of imagination, and only possessed by the few complete artists of the world. Michael Angelo possessed it; but he was surrounded by accessible living models, and could constantly refer to them. Rimmer had no models, and never in all his life employed one more than an hour or two at a time. How long or faithfully he worked from his female models on the DEATH OF ABEL picture cannot be determined; but, if the habit of his later art life is any correct standard of judgment, it could not have been long.

He drew upon any scrap of paper that came within his reach. At times, the floor of the room, wherever he might be, would be strewn with drawings of every possible subject, grave, gay, grotesque, poetic, and illustrative. Neither time, place, nor circumstance seriously affected in any way his disposition for continuous work. The luxuries of a well-appointed studio he never enjoyed. Possibly it would have made no difference with him. Wherever he could get a pencil, paint, brushes and canvas, was his studio. "He painted on the floor in the sitting-room," says one of the family, "in the hall-way, on the stairs, or in the attic."

Nothing disturbed him while at work. The noise and antics of his grandchildren, an argument with a friend, or a discourse upon some art, political, or social subject, very often occupied him while he was busy with his work.

The majority of the drawings exhibited at the Art Museum in 1880 were made under these circumstances, and owe their preservation to the fact that members of his family would bring him the leaf of an album or other piece of paper, in order that they might save now and then a drawing of the mass that otherwise would go to the rag-bag.

Dr. Rimmer spent his summers in some quiet town in the country, but was always busy painting or drawing, very often accompanied by one or two pupils. The walks and mountain-climbing of himself and family were generally delineated in some grotesque or humoristic way. It may be imagined that he was a master of caricature, an amusement in which he indulged only on these occasions. Had he chosen to employ his genius either as an illustrator or caricaturist, he would have become famous. He seldom, if ever, used a sketch-book, but relied upon his memory for the preservation of every thing he desired to use in his delineations. He was fond of animals, especially lions; and he made many sketches of them. The coming of a menagerie was a longed-for and much-enjoyed feast.

Many of Dr. Rimmer's compositions remind one of Blake, — the two natures being widely dissimilar, yet with many resemblances. Rimmer was more terrestrial, and understood the human figure better. He lived on the earth, and believed in it, although he soared above it. Blake lived above it all the time, and used it as something subordinate. Rimmer's figures are solid and weighty: they rest. Blake's figures are on the earth, not because they belong to it, but simply to illustrate a fact or sentiment. He did not recognize the world as we see it: he lived among celestial visions. Rimmer did recognize it, even if he looked down upon it.

*The Flight of Night*, and *The Discoverer*, are taken from charcoal-sketches of pictures painted upon the walls of the Assembly Chamber in the New York State Capitol at Albany, by the late William M. Hunt. They are the only large pictures or important compositions made by Rimmer's chief contemporary in Boston.

The illustrations from Millet, Blake, and Michael Angelo are selected for the purpose of comparison. No greater extremes, perhaps, could exist than those between Rimmer and Millet. The beauty and power resulting from a sympathy with and a constant intimate study of the human figure is strikingly illustrated by the sketch of *Falling Figures* by Michael Angelo. The charm, fulness, and poetry of the illustrations from the Book of Job, by William Blake, can hardly be too warmly appreciated.

## CHAPTER XX.

### CONCLUSION.

DR. RIMMER wrote in his diary this singular sentence: " I have practised art all my life to gratify my family, or in gratitude for some one's friendship."

Taken in connection with the events of his life, these words will explain to many the unevenness of his art career, the incompleteness of its success, and will diminish the affectionate remembrance ever given to those artists who have found their chief pleasure under all circumstances in the undeviatingly loyal and self-sacrificing pursuit of their art.

To others it will add a superior title to human distinction, and a warmer appreciation of him as a man. To them it would absolve him from criticism as an artist, except in the case of his connection with the execution of public work.

At first thought it seems an unexpected declaration.

If no more sympathetic wish could be expressed in admiration of his genius than that he might have known the art souls of ancient and modern times, so there is no fact in his life so tantalizing to an artist as that he made no effort to this end. The regret that he did not almost equals the admiration for what he succeeded in doing without such inspiring and transforming intimacy. With strong minds a capacity for progress implies an uncontrollable desire for its attainment, and a self-sacrifice oftentimes amounting to cruelty.

This capacity he possessed in a sufficient degree to enable him to go through a great deal of hard study with a perseverance as rare as it is splendid, and to exceed, more than any other artist of his time, the limited facilities of his immediate locality. But it is one of the anomalies in the history of artists, that a man with so strong an art sense should have had a love of domestic life so much

130

56. **Morning—Male Figure**

stronger. I do not understand that he was particularly, if at all, interested in the lives, temperaments, or works of the principal artists of his own generation, or that he had the desire of professional sympathy or soulful identification common to the imaginative temperament; at least, no wish sufficiently strong to urge him to make at any cost even a short visit to the living art-centres of the Old World.

He had art knowledge and genius enough to conquer not only any and all the untoward circumstances of his life, but to establish an era of art in this country. But he accepted circumstances, and followed the bent of his own nature and feelings, whether towards art or away from it. If the results were disastrous, he made no complaint. In certain matters one's own way is heroism. His home was at all times a never-failing joy. He felt art in all its varied phases, and touched, perhaps unconsciously, every one of its mighty chords.

I say unconsciously; because I must believe, that had he really known their vast meaning, their resounding power, their majestic consolation, their imposing obligatory response, he would have entered into an extravagant exercise of them, despite all difficulties, and made his domestic happiness a still greater joy, as well as an auxiliary to a fuller art life. For a man capable of so much to know, that, for reasons beyond his control, he cannot do his best, is one of the bitterest inflictions that helpless humanity is forced to endure.

That such a nature as his should appear in this country when it did, is one of the strange, sad facts which from time to time appear in American life; which are difficult to explain, yet which invigorate every one of its phases, and which alone preserve its art from an easily forgotten death. What Dr. Rimmer did accomplish has a double value, and it will receive in due season its just tribute from every sincere artist and man.

# SUPPLEMENT.

THE opinions and critical estimates expressed by those who knew Dr. Rimmer, in regard to his character, his powers, and the value of his teachings, are so curiously conflicting, that I give a few of them, leaving the reader to weigh and digest them for himself. They are for the most part written by his pupils, or by artists who knew him, and are valuable as helping to the formation of an accurate judgment of Dr. Rimmer's real nature and worth.

---

"Dr. Rimmer's lectures, in my humble opinion, were valuable in supplying a theoretical knowledge of drawing, the practical knowledge of which, in studying from the nude model, was unattainable by art students in general. It was well as far as it went, and doubtless has prepared the public to sustain, as well as to tolerate, such an enterprise as the Students' Art League in New York."

---

"I held Dr. Rimmer in high esteem as a teacher. He came as near my ideal of a teacher as any one I have known, in his kindly sympathy, encouragement, and guidance, and in his honestly expressed criticism."

---

"I never drew, or tried to follow closely, the figures that the doctor made on the board. The man claimed and received all my attention. He seemed to feel, draw, and talk over the heads of his audience. His observations were clear and explicit, but there was something in it all that was outside of the moment. He impressed me as far greater than the task that occupied him. He was capable of regaling ripe artists, and should never have been obliged to exhibit himself as a pictorial circus to the common student. His lectures were intellectual repasts."

---

"I never knew a man so well of whom I can say so little. Personally he inspired you, but it did not last. Have known him for a great many years, and he has been in my studio from time to time. The exhibition of his works at the Art Museum was as great a surprise to me as it was to others."

---

"His teaching of figure-drawing was something which could not be had even in Europe, and he was master of what he taught. What the A B C is to every grown person, anatomy was to him; and not only the structure of the human frame, and placing of muscles and tendons, but their position and change in motion. He was very patient, only occasionally showing what he must often have felt, how poorly the spirit of his drawing was comprehended. For any students who had their work at heart, his teaching was invaluable. We were always sorry to see the cloth wipe away a spirited drawing, and finally a few were photographed. He was of a most kindly nature, of pleasant manners, and liked to talk on many subjects besides art. If he could have known, ten or twenty years sooner, the great powers that lay dormant while he patiently worked as physician, his life would have been easier, and much trouble would have been spared him. He might then have found time to go to Europe, and see the pictures and sculpture which he knew by heart from engravings and copies."

---

"His teaching excited me as nothing of the sort had ever done before. He tried to get us to draw on the board, but we didn't make a practice of it. He also wished us to model small statues in clay, out of hours, and bring them to him for correction. Not much of that was done; but he made the class bring him a good many original drawings, exemplifying the rules and information he had given us. These drawings he liked to have us invent. When we brought him drawings, he used first to criticise them before the class: afterward, when there were fewer students, he allowed us to bring them to him after the hours of instruction. He did not like us to work in charcoal, I think; nor did he give us any great affection for the values of light and shade in themselves, though he did tell us about light and shade somewhat. He liked us to work in red and black crayon. He said one should never use black or white paper: it was too violent. He preferred having us use colored paper with black crayon. Most of the drawings we brought him were done in black-lead pencil. Of course, all the work we did in class was pencil outline, unless, as rarely happened, he did a little light-and-shade work for us, which was done with charcoal and chalk on the dark-gray slate of the blackboard. I do not think, although I may be mistaken, that he thought constant study from nature a very important thing for us. He himself was so full of ideas, that I believe he half expected us to feel so too. His anatomical explanations were beautifully clear, even to young, ignorant girls. We became wild with excitement about the deltoid muscle, and, indeed, the rest of them; but he didn't allow us — at least he did not wish us — to have our attention too much fixed on details of that sort. 'Morbid anatomy,' as he called it, was his horror; and it seems to me, that, valuable as was his general teaching, his rules for blocking out figures, and for considering at first nothing but action and proportion, are the most valuable parts of it. Uninteresting and vulgar detail, he made us despise; and though he kept our minds fixed on the figure, and its form and action, to such an extent that our ideal was a narrow one, it was not his fault if it were not a very high and noble one. Spirit and feeling were what he most cared for, and what made him forgive a great many faults in his scholars' work."

---

"He was great as a lecturer on art anatomy, but not a thorough teacher of drawing, painting, or sculpture. He lacked taste, and could not always distinguish between good and bad. He did not rightly appreciate study from nature, prizing unduly what he called 'ideal work.' He was sensitive and sometimes irritable, and unfitted to work with others."

---

"He taught what he knew, not what the various temperaments of the art nature needed as circumstanced at this time in New England."

---

"He would begin with the toe at the top of the board, and run down through a number of figures as fast as he could handle the chalk, — so fast that one could scarcely tell when one figure was done and another begun. The NINE DAYS THEY FELL was one of an interminable number of groups made upon the blackboard. He seemed like a romancer, who, out of an unknown world, strung an endless procession of noble forms. His nature was very refined, but impracticable and queer."

---

"When I heard Dr. Rimmer lecture in Worcester, I received the impression — and it clings to me now — that some of his alleged 'impracticability' lay in a public not sufficiently lenient and sympathetic, and too closely wedded to immobile artistic standards. If an artist's imagination persists in working eccentrically, or contrary to our assumptions, if it be strong, manly, and serious, and the artist himself has firm faith in it, why try to bind him to our plough, and make him walk in our furrow? If we do not enjoy his productions ourselves, let us cherish them. Dr. Rimmer's peculiar idealism had a most direct influence upon his life and work. It made him proud, repelling, very dependent upon himself and his family. He lived in solitude, brooding over his own conceptions. His work became extraordinarily individual. It is not like any thing else at all. It is always strong, often repulsive. He firmly believed in his own unaided imagination, as a straight and direct road to the ideal. To receive the influence of others' work, to bend to the courses of contemporary thoughts and doings, to be artistically sympathetic, was impossible. To be bold, virile, pugnacious, unconditional, critical, was a necessity to him.

"Dr. Rimmer was as successful in the expression of animal nature as in any thing. His conception of the brute was superb. It was, doubtless, not the thing of which he approved as an ideal, nor what he considered the best object of his thoughts and study. It was nevertheless just the thing in which his imagination found itself most unprejudiced, and the least trammelled by theory. With the exception of one or two of Barye's pieces, and the Assyrian bas-reliefs, I know of no more powerful conceptions of animal ferocity than the FIGHTING LIONS. The doctor's CENTAUR is quite unique, and without a peer. The doubling-back of the horse, the terrible writhing of the animal part, has never been expressed in any such way before. To be sure, the torso is mannered to a certain degree; but its attachment to the horse is extraordinarily clever, and its ideal character only serves to contrast it the more perfectly with the beast, — to which it is welded.

"Rarely in the history of art has a professed idealist carried into his work such intensity of feeling and such strength of imagination. Canova certainly did not. His Italian *Boxers* are mere oxen compared to Rimmer's GLADIATOR. Dr. Rimmer's feelings did not seem to need the stimulus which the realist derives from contact with nature. It must always be regretted that he was not born in an artistic community, acquainted with technical conditions, and skilled in the manipulation of material.

"In his best moods his imagination could force its way through the greatest obstacles, but stuff which he handled often annoyed and hampered him. That which the younger generation of American artists learns at the beginning, and perhaps enjoys too keenly at times, was, for the most part, ignored by him. That Dr. Rimmer completed so little, will be regretted more hereafter than it is now; but the little which remains is so much more vigorous, manly, and imaginative than the productions which surround it, that I am accustomed to look upon him as perhaps the only sculptor of his generation in America who will be considered a great artist in our artistic period — when that shall come. That another equally individual shall appear, is to be hoped for, but not expected. One at least of Dr. Rimmer's pupils remembers him with a respect and admiration, which, from the first, has not abated. That he was mighty is true; and that he will one day be known is certain."

58. WATER-COLOR SKETCH

57. THE MASTER BUILDER

"There can be no doubt that Dr. Rimmer had the most profound knowledge of art, and an intuitive feeling and love for the grand and high forms of expression. No one could listen to him without admiration, and a feeling of being raised nearer to his high standard."

---

"The faults of the doctor's method were, that he did not sufficiently regard the individual nature of his pupils, the necessity of acquiring art knowledge from nature at the very start, and its constant employment by pupils in their studies. The subtle, sympathetic, and mysterious charm, the tone of nature, Dr. Rimmer did not recognize. He seemed to approach nature as an antagonist, — to conquer its individuality for his art purpose, as a shipbuilder goes into a forest to cut down the monarchs of a century."

---

"He was stubborn and unmanageable. In spite of the unartistic condition of things about him, he was his own worst enemy. He expected princes and kings to come to him. He should have lived in an age when he could have produced any thing that he pleased, without suggestion, domination, or necessity. The slightest thing put him out. He could have no relation with anybody. Poverty and neglect not only depressed him, but stopped his art. Even when he had a chance, he failed to do his best. He was never popular with the public or artists."

---

"His idea of tone in a picture was, that whatever color was selected as the key should be used always, with more or less intensity, with other colors, all through the work. He found fault with other painters because they neglected this idea."

---

One of the best artists in this country writes as follows: "In facility of drawing, in power of composition, and in comprehension of the human figure, alone or together, I know of no artist in history who could excel him. I have often asked him to begin a toe on one corner of the board, a finger on another, and so on, until the parts of several figures were begun. Then I would ask him to put in the remainder of the figures, which he would do with the most astonishing readiness and correctness.

"He said that sometimes a whole figure was suggested to him by a chance mark upon the blackboard; that he was utterly unconscious at times of what he was going to do the next moment; and that he was assisted in a composition by the remembrance of the component parts that he had not thought of for years. Every thing that he saw took its proper place in his memory, and came at his unconscious call when needed.

"Whatever merit his works at the Museum may possess, they are mannered and dry in comparison with the drawings made in his classes. There, he never seemed to me to be conscious of what he was doing, or was capable of doing. Away from the blackboard, he seemed conscious, and even pretentious. He never accomplished any thing like as much good in teaching as he would have done if he could have had work to do. In some respects he was an extraordinary teacher; in others, he was too much of a *doctrinaire*. He had too much of the receipt, — one plan for all. No man could arouse more interest in the human figure than did Dr. Rimmer. He was a guide, not a teacher. He had not sufficient art education to warrant his assuming to teach art. He did not seem to realize this.

"He was praised too much. He needed work without restrictions, and plenty of it. If the Bostonians interested in art had given him work, let him choose his own subjects, and not disturbed his former habits of life, he would have done marvellous things. But the disposition to find genius, and trot it out to gratify a notoriety, is characteristic of Boston. I know that there are those who think that Dr. Rimmer had not the capacity to produce a complete work; that he had none of that force necessary for a concentrated effort of long duration; that he could not be relied on, was erratic and stubborn, that he was quickly outside of his subject. But that is Bostonian. Bostonians never look square at a man's work: they want to know about its perspective, its drawing, and whether it has been sanctioned by foreigners. They never see or care for the possibilities of an artist, or the suggestive character of his work. They want talk. They run one artist at a time. Look at Hunt, for instance. Who they will take up next, I can't imagine. Rimmer was not at all fitted for any general relation with men. He was in the air. All Rimmer needed was the assistance to produce something, — no matter what. He ought to have been taken hold of as a sculptor. Perhaps no one is to blame because he was not.

"This eagerness to learn about art, the mania for art schools, lectures, experiments, and systems, is not an evidence of a general interest in art: it rather indicates that it is believed that art can be taught and learned; that it is merely the acquiring of something. The producers are a secondary consideration; and yet they are the basis of all true art progress. Hunt was right when he said, 'There is too much talk about art;' but he said it in vain.

"Production is the great thing. The art instinct is not understood in New England, and is not likely to be for some time. We never study its nature, and consequently have no judgment of our own. The responsiveness to art is the negative one of culture, which is at best slow, and never certain of itself. What good has all the twenty years' teaching of Hunt and Rimmer done? None. There is not the enthusiasm there used to be, and no independence of perception and judgment. We use borrowed opinion. Boston art interest has died down to exhibitions.

"Rimmer disliked to lecture; but, being obliged to, he did it with as much enthusiasm as he could. Personally, he did not impress me. His pictures were not agreeable, and his work generally is fragmentary and unsatisfactory."

" He did not give so much as he awakened.   He confirmed one in the great things which were dimly one's own.   He talked from the centre of things.   He rejoiced in his work.   I did not care for him as a person ; but I felt that as an artist he was great, great, great ! "

---

" He had no times as other men in art had.   There was no art life : in him not even its birth had taken place.   He relied upon the force of his own nature.   He was a man of strong convictions, but of no extraordinary intelligence outside of art."

---

" The keynote to all Dr. Rimmer's instruction was form ; good position and relation of parts.   To the pupil who could not grasp this central and vital truth, the instruction was ever blind, impracticable, incomprehensible.

" To vulgarity and pretence, in every shade of existence, he was most intolerant ; and none detected it in its incipient stage quicker than he.

" To honest endeavor, accompanied with true artistic humility, he was more than helpful : he was encouraging, hopeful, and inspiring."

---

" On the day of Senator Sumner's funeral in Washington, the doctor selected the subject of grief, and gave it an exhaustive oral and pictorial illustration.   Morning and evening were favorite subjects of delineation.   There seemed to be no limit to the variety of his conception of these very suggestive subjects, nor of the means by which they might be expressed.   Evening was often represented by a beautiful female figure descending upon the earth ; and morning, by a crowd of cherubs, sailing in vigorous gladness through the sky, with lighted torches.

" On entering the schoolroom he would often go to the blackboard, and draw a face or head, or a female figure, saying, 'I saw this in the car ; ' and proceed to comment upon it at length.   He would often draw the heads of pupils to illustrate taste, style, etc.

" After drawing and lessons in anatomy, — 'dry bones,' as some called these hours, — he would give us some delightful cupids floating upon clouds, 'Morning' and 'Evening,' or some strange warlike figure ; something to appeal to the imagination ; and he would say, 'There, put that into your books : make ideal drawings, charcoal, pencil, red chalk, oil-colors ; use whatever medium you best like ; but try to acquire the power of expressing yourselves.   Think of sentiment, type, style, light and shade, and, above all, of correct outline.'

" Hunt said of Rimmer, 'What the doctor does is not drawing,' referring to his blackboard-work, and while he was illustrating his own idea of drawing by masses.   Rimmer said, 'The trouble with Hunt is, that he cannot draw,' alluding to the *Boy and the Butter-*

*fly*.  Hunt urged his pupils to go to Rimmer, and learn anatomy, and would say, 'Almost everybody hates Rimmer's things.  I don't: I like them.'

"Looking at a picture by one of Mr. Hunt's pupils, the doctor observed, 'There is a good deal of good in that, but it is a dangerous thing for an amateur to do.  Those who paint like that must be old hands who have forgotten their early teaching; masters, not pupils.  He imitates a well-known painter.  This style of work can only be done by a master.  Mr. Hunt, in order to do this, has learned all the details and facts, and can now dare to do things like these.' "

---

"Some quality seems to have been lacking in Rimmer's organization; perhaps it was an ever-present sense of ideal beauty, which, had it but kept pace with his power of expression, would have left him without a rival in ancient or modern times."

---

"He came to public notice when he was too old to hold public attention, and begin work.  Had he been younger, the result would have been different."

---

"He had none of the qualities that win a wide popularity.  By his morbid sensitiveness and extraordinary standard of judging men, he lessened the number of his friends, and put himself voluntarily at variance with that courteous charity, that, by common consent and the necessity of common existence, keeps society together.  He put nature and the world at defiance; not that he might more peacefully enter into their innocent and chaste souls as a minstrel in receptive sympathy, but as a proud ruler.  His experience and study were in consequence limited and self-consuming.  He could not bear criticism, but he judged others unsparingly.  What he would have accomplished in an art-centre like Paris, I cannot imagine.  If he was not the recipient of public encouragement, it was his own fault.  Certainly he possessed an unusual knowledge among artists in America, but he knew nothing of men.  He is great, very great in some respects, as an artist; but as a man among men he gave no evidence of more than common ability.  It is what a man accomplishes, that sustains a claim to permanent regard, no matter how or where he works.  His opportunities were by no means poor.  He would not, or could not, embrace them.  Neither men nor nature charmed him.

"It is said that 'joys impregnate; sorrows bring forth;' and this is the surest test of a great mind in art.  Men like Millet and Barye wrung masterpieces out of their sorrow and poverty; but these experiences had no such effect upon Rimmer.  He succeeded none, and none will succeed him.  He had neither youth nor motive, and made little progress."

"Dr. Rimmer had too little appreciation of the difficulties that beset beginners. His method was better for genius than mediocrity, but not fitted for such a school as the Cooper Institute. His kindness and helpfulness were endless and unfailing."

---

"He was conceited and overbearing, — must be the highest and first, or nothing. He turned out all the other teachers at the Institute, and was finally obliged to follow them. He was popular among favorite pupils, and would let them do as they pleased. No one instructor, however great, can conduct a school of so large a number of students as attended the Institute. His peculiar temperament caused him to dislike many good people; and, as a natural consequence, he was disliked by them. A great school does not depend upon one man. No thoroughly great artist would have undertaken what Rimmer did."

---

"He was a wonder. He had great projects, and, if he had not been crushed by poverty and misfortune in his early life, would undoubtedly have accomplished great things. He had a right to be proud; but he could not manage circumstances, nor govern his feelings. He lacked repose, the essential quality of all great and well-balanced artists. After all, Rimmer is to be remembered for what he was, and what he did; not for what he was not, or what he did not do."

---

"His lectures on the various topics embraced in the programme of the Cooper Institute were as learned in science as they were masterly in art. He was familiar with all the expressions of human and animal nature. In my long residence in the art-countries of Europe, I have never been more impressed by any artist's versatility and profound knowledge. If the drawings of entire figures, and compositions of figures, that Dr. Rimmer drew on the blackboard at the Cooper Institute could have been preserved, as they ought to have been, they would have made an invaluable and wonderful contribution to American art. The memory of Dr. Rimmer's instruction never ceases to inspire me. He gave himself to his pupils without stint, especially to those who were earnest: to amateurs, and those whose money was their only recommendation, he was utterly unhelpful and indifferent; and they consequently gave untrue reports of his method and instruction, and very often became his enemies. His perceptions were so keen as to seem like something supernatural. He had great respect for different temperaments and individual characteristics. His interest in his pupils was without limit. If he thought they could not succeed as artists, he would advise them to take up some other profession. This, too, would give offence. He was easily disturbed, and an uncongenial person annoyed him greatly. Michael Angelo and Dr. Rimmer are inseparable in my mind. He was too great for an instructor at the Cooper Institute."

" He did not keep his pupils well enough in hand. It was folly to permit persons to compose, paint, and model what they pleased, before they could draw. This I found to my cost after I went to Europe."

---

" Dr. Rimmer did not carry his work far enough. Whether this was from lack of patience or early training, I know not. He impressed me as a sculptor, rather than as a painter. His task at the Cooper Institute was enormous, too great for a well man. He was overworked, and suffered from ill health, oftentimes from great depression. His kindness was unlimited. He had undoubted genius; and, could he have lived in Europe, he would have become illustrious."

---

" Dr. Rimmer was a grand teacher for talented and hard-working students of art. He had enemies among his pupils. They were generally the incapable and indolent. He could not bear dictation from any source, and occasionally there was trouble."

---

" He had, I think, a great deal of influence at the Cooper Institute. Many of the young women there were from the West and the country, poor, and often uneducated. Dr. Rimmer had a peculiar kindness for these, and used sometimes to lecture to them in off-hours upon astronomy, in which he was interested. He had a rough manner, and that strange sense, that it was necessary to assert himself with people who were well-bred, that one finds sometimes among the Americans of a certain class: this, and a great love of money, caused him to do very grasping things. He had really a kind heart, and a strong admiration of talent, which he was never slow to recognize. Indeed, I think his standard was not high enough: that which was anatomical he called beautiful. I think that many of Dr. Rimmer's pupils are far better fitted than I am to give you personal accounts of him: but I also think that none could feel more grateful for his instructions than I do, or more eager to testify to the worth of his teaching in anatomy; but, as a general instructor in art, I thought him superficial and dangerous."

---

" Like a good physician, he was interested in the health of his pupils. ' You must not sit here so long,' he would say to one or another who was in the habit of remaining late at work in the afternoon; and he gave one short but serious lecture to the whole school on the use and abuse of anæsthetics, called out by his having learned that some of the young ladies had taken laughing-gas in the dentist's room below."

59. FROM THE BOOK OF JOB

"His influence, it seems to me, is seen in the best work of Mary Hallock Foote, and others, who, like her, drew enthusiasm from him."

———————

"It was not in our work that he helped us, so much as in teaching us to see things."

———————

"He wanted every impression to go through the influence of the imagination."

———————

"There always seemed to me something particularly noble in the fearless way in which Dr. Rimmer would answer, 'I do not know,' when questions were asked about matters which he had not studied."

———————

"He had a way of saying 'child' to a favorite pupil; and I sometimes thought he considered all of us Cooper Institute girls as his children, and so treated us in the tender way he treated his own family."

———————

"He had no fondness for general society, saying that the atmosphere of most people oppressed him; although, to those whom he did find congenial, he was most strongly attracted."

———————

"His constant cry as he passed a pupil was, 'Work, work, work!'"

———————

"He was exceedingly sensitive, observed the slightest tone or manner of a person, was grave in his behavior, and had great regard for the dignity of his character."

———————

"He hated any thing like sham, whether in art or in people. He was not a politic man. Complaint was sometimes made that at the Cooper Institute, he did not pay proper deference to the trustees. I have always had the opinion that his leaving the Institute arose from his unwillingness to pay deference to ignorance. His was a manly character in every sense. He seemed annoyed whenever he encountered any one below his own standard of what was just and proper. He was proud of the progress of his pupils, and sensitive to any unjust criticism of their work.  His nature was too large to complain, and he had no bitterness against the world.  He delighted in retirement, and courted a tranquillity far from the uneasiness of modern life.  He relied upon himself; read a great deal, but studied no particular artist; never sought praise or popularity.

" He often said, ' I believe in the genius of work and in the diversity of art talent; and, if an artist does not keep himself above the natural actuality of his subject, whether of poetry, music, painting, or sculpture, he will become weakened by its influence.'  He liked to look from a height down upon subjects and men.  He had great faith in the integrity of the working-classes, and often said that ' no people in the world will give a quicker or more generous response to suffering, the cause of right, or justice, than Americans.'  He advocated trusting the people to govern, and preparing them to govern themselves."

———————

" In giving you my impressions of the works of the late Dr. William Rimmer, I am fully aware of the fact, that the greatest things in art are so subtle, that words, as a medium of their translation, become gross and unwieldy; and to analyze the art-life of Dr. Rimmer, seems almost impossible.  Therefore I venture but a few remarks, drawn from my recollection of his works (more especially his drawings) taken as a whole, and not in detail.

" In Dr. Rimmer we see a man brought up in a new country, where every thing is crude and unfinished, and art a mere affectation, living in a commercial age, when the very air is stifling to art, seeking to express himself before a cold and unsympathetic world.  He finds himself alone.

" You know full well that men who produce great and original things in art, even under most favorable circumstances, are rare; and, of the thousands in the world who have to do with art, few can lay valid claim to great respect, and of whom it can be justly said, that they have produced works that will last and be admired more and more as the centuries roll on.

" In Dr. Rimmer we see a man, who, in the face of most adverse circumstances, actually does something that challenges the admiration of artists and laymen, and establishes the fact that he possesses an artistic temperament.  Such a result, in this country, is certainly extraordinary.  There are those who do clever, pleasing things in art, — things that perhaps show great mastery over material.  Such men are not rare.  But those who produce, or even indicate by the slightest touch of pencil or chisel a latent power to produce, things big and grand in art, — such men are few; and Dr. Rimmer was one of these.  When the history of the early development of art in this country shall be written, his name will occupy a high place, and his work receive serious consideration.  I do homage to this man's genius."

The following extract from a letter written by an eminent English artist to "The Examiner" of June, 1867, of Manchester, England, is one of the many specimens of foreign appreciation of Dr. Rimmer's abilities while connected with the Cooper Institute : —

"None give any idea of the artists' scope. I have yet, perhaps, to say the same of American art. But if I speak of it — so far as I have seen — as generally young and crude, and not sufficiently self-reliant, I must reverse all that in speaking of a GLADIATOR by Dr. Rimmer, — a life-size statue, treated realistically, not classically, the muscles shown in detail (not exaggerated, but delicately, in their contours and insertions), rather than in the more ideal breadth of the antique method. Yet it is a statue deserving to be compared with the antique. Of how many modern works can we say so much ? You will not tire your fingers in endeavoring to count. Dr. Rimmer is a man of, I suppose, over fifty, a physician, and excellent anatomist ; and this statue is but his second work, — his first a head of ST. STEPHEN, cut in granite. He is now modelling, in the classic style, a full-length figure of ORPHEUS (singing against the Sirens), not unlike in conception to Raffaelle's *Apollo contending with Marsyas.* Dr. Rimmer is the lecturer on anatomy and master at the Ladies' (free) School of Design at the Cooper Institute in this city, — an institute founded and endowed by Peter Cooper, to provide certain free schools, a free library, and lecture-rooms. I have gone through the School of Design, and heard some of the course of lectures on anatomy. Of the first, I must say that it is the only school of design in which I have seen drawing thoroughly taught ; and of the lectures, I can but report that they are the most profoundly considered and systematically arranged, and, at the same time, the most lucidly-delivered lectures it ever fell to my lot to hear. The GLADIATOR and the school are the best things I have found here yet."

---

In a private letter, the same writer says : —

"Rimmer had in him all the elements of a great artist. Any shortcoming I take to be due to the time given to another profession. Art is too jealous a mistress to allow of any attention elsewhere. Yet, as his GLADIATOR shows, his thorough anatomical knowledge was of vast assistance to him. As a teacher, I have known none to equal him. His lectures at the Institute were only to his class. I was once, however, allowed to be present ; and if that lecture was a fair sample of the course, I can but lament that every thing in that way coming from him has not been preserved, blackboard illustrations included. A ready and excellent draughtsman, a full and easy speaker, I, having heard many lectures in my time, have never heard one so accomplished. Two subjects had been selected for him — as was, I believe, the custom — by his pupils, — Windmills, and the Varieties of Animal Form. He gave a clear and comprehensive history of mills, wind and water, with illustrations ; then, passing to the animals, drew a number of most characteristic heads, beginning with the skull, pointing out differences, and explaining, of course, as he went on.  So much, and such varied information, so easily given in one short hour, I never heard from any one else.

"What his real nature was, — when you could see beyond a sensitive shyness that made many think him brusque and indisposed to friendliness, — I do not hesitate to affirm.  Short — too short for my own desire — as the time of our friendship was, I can speak positively of that. I think I have known no man more manly, true, kindly, and religious, in the highest degree of the word.  I am sure that others who had the advantage of longer and more intimate intercourse with him will confirm what I say.  Not only as an artist, but as a man, all the elements of greatness were in him; and there was a rare mixture of imagination — as in Blake, and shown in his poetry, of which, I suppose, nothing has been published, but he read fragments to me occasionally — with clear sense, and a power of practical action.  A most remarkable man, of high genius, however the full development of that may have been hindered by circumstances.  Not all acquainted with him knew him.  The more there is in a man, the more difficult it is to get at him.  I may add that Dr. Rimmer was not known either in Boston or New York, either by the public generally — his reserved habits keeping him out of society — or by the artist-world, else his standing and circumstances had been very different.  I hold no test to my own estimate of him, and will not abate one jot of admiration for the artist, or of admiring affection for the man.  His works speak for themselves."

---

"Dr. Rimmer had full faith in the necessity of drawing from the life model, but did not believe in allowing the pupil to do so until a knowledge of the principles of anatomy enabled him to understand what he was doing.  'As well,' he would say, 'to set a person down to read a foreign language before he has learned the value of the letters which compose the words, as to ask a person to draw a human figure without some knowledge of the bones and muscles which compose it.'  In connection with the habit of observation, he laid great stress on memory sketching.  'Take a good look at something that you see in the street, in the house, anywhere, — a rag-picker stooping over an ash-barrel; a woman lifting a child in her arms; any thing, anybody: try and photograph it, so to speak, on the mind, and then draw it from memory.  In this way you will learn to seize only the salient points of every thing, discarding all that is superfluous.'  In regard to grouping, he said, 'Remember that in a properly balanced group every figure is a necessary part of it, and the removal of even the most insignificant would be disastrous to the harmony of the whole.  Grouping does not consist in standing figures in a row like pins in a paper, nor in sticking them over the surface of the picture like pins in a cushion: they must be arranged so as to lead the eye by a natural gradation to the principal figure, and every thing else must serve the same end, — the arrangement of the light and shade, the disposition of the draperies, the combination of color, which should be most prominent and striking around the central point of interest.'"

60. FLIGHT AND PURSUIT

61. ACHILLES

COURTESY, MUSEUM OF FINE ARTS, BOSTON; GIFT OF E. W. HOOPER, W. S. BIGELOW, AND MRS. JOHN M. FORBES.

"An atmosphere of color was one thing upon which he insisted. 'It is not enough to bring a red dress and a blue cloak together, — any dry-goods clerk can do that: you must do more than this, — you must make them acquainted, nay, friendly with each other. You must bring them into a loving embrace, each borrowing from and adding to the beauty of the other; the warmth of the red softening the coolness of the blue, the purity and tenderness of the blue mellowing the fierce glow of the red, and the gray of the atmosphere tempering both. There should be a little of one color in every other color, and a little of every other color in one color. Talk of transparency! some people seem to think they have secured it when you can see the canvas through the paint: they forget that you do not want the transparency of glass that you can see through, but of jewels you can see into. Always have one central effect of color to which every thing else is subordinated. Do not be afraid to sacrifice the others to it: reverse the order of sacrificing one to the good of many, and make many suffer to give proper value to one. Remember the maxim, that color is tone. The massing together of fine colors without regard to their harmony does not constitute good color, any more than the putting-on of fine garments without regard to their fitness constitutes good dressing. Color should always assist in expressing the sentiment of the subject. A musician does not compose a funeral march to a waltz tune, nor a song of triumph to the same measure as a plaint of sorrow; nor should a painter. He should clothe his subject in color as in a garment: joy, love, triumph, should glow in a golden glory amid pure and brilliant hues, the blaze of jewels, and the glitter of gold and silver. Not so grief, despair, defeat: to them belong the garb of woe, the sombre robe and sable plume; and, though it may be well to introduce a brighter or a happier tint, it should be but to point more vividly to the actual tone of the picture, just as a rift of clear blue in a stormy sky makes more apparent the blackness of the thunder-clouds. Avoid gaudiness and heat while you strive for richness and warmth. Remember, too, that harmony is quite compatible with variety of color; but, on the other hand, avoid crowding too many distinct colors into your picture, as though you were offering your audience a sample lot of ribbons. Above all, remember atmosphere, that impalpable something which we feel but do not see, which softens every defect, and throws over every thing a thin, transparent veil.'"